Macaroni & Cheese

Publications International, Ltd.
Favorite Brand Name Recipes at www.fbnr.com

ISBN-13: 978-1-4127-9785-6
ISBN-10: 1-4127-9785-3

Library of Congress Control Number: 2009920138

Manufactured in China.

8 7 6 5 4 3 2 1

Microwave Cooking: Microwave ovens vary in wattage. Use the cooking times as guidelines and check for doneness before adding more time.

Preparation/Cooking Times: Preparation times are based on the approximate amount of time required to assemble the recipe before cooking, baking, chilling or serving. These times include preparation steps such as measuring, chopping and mixing. The fact that some preparations and cooking can be done simultaneously is taken into account. Preparation of optional ingredients and serving suggestions is not included.

Contents

Stovetop Mac & Cheese. 4

Baked Mac & Cheese 32

Fancy Mac & Cheese 66

Shortcut Mac & Cheese 94

Beyond Mac & Cheese 116

Acknowledgments. 139

Index 140

Stovetop Mac & Cheese

Stovetop Macaroni and Cheese

Makes 6 servings

1 tablespoon salt
12 ounces elbow macaroni, uncooked
1 (12-ounce) can evaporated milk
¼ cup **CREAM OF WHEAT**® Hot Cereal (Instant, 1-minute, 2½-minute or 10-minute cook time), uncooked
2 eggs
1 teaspoon Dijon mustard
½ teaspoon **TRAPPEY'S**® Red Devil™ Cayenne Pepper Sauce
½ teaspoon salt
8 ounces Cheddar cheese, shredded
½ cup milk

1. Bring large pot of water to a boil. Stir in salt. Add macaroni. Stir, then cook 8 minutes or until tender. Drain and return pasta to pot.

2. While pasta is cooking, whisk evaporated milk, Cream of Wheat, eggs, mustard, pepper sauce and salt in medium bowl.

3. Add mixture to cooked pasta. Cook and stir over medium-low heat until mixture thickens. Gradually stir in cheese, adding more as it melts. Add ½ cup milk; stir until creamy. Serve warm.

PREP TIME: 5 minutes
COOK TIME: 15 to 20 minutes

TIP: For a nice garnish and to add some extra crunch to this old favorite, combine ¼ cup fresh bread crumbs with ¼ cup Cream of Wheat. Melt 1 tablespoon butter in small saucepan over medium heat. Add Cream of Wheat mixture; cook and stir until mixture is golden brown. Sprinkle on top of each serving.

Fettuccine alla Carbonara

Makes 4 servings

12 ounces uncooked fettuccine or spaghetti
 4 ounces pancetta or bacon, cut crosswise into ½-inch-wide strips
 3 cloves garlic, cut into halves
¼ cup dry white wine
⅓ cup whipping cream
 1 egg
 1 egg yolk
⅔ cup grated Parmesan cheese, divided
   Dash white pepper

1. Cook fettuccine according to package directions. Drain well; cover and keep warm.

2. Cook and stir pancetta and garlic in large skillet over medium-low heat 4 minutes or until pancetta is lightly browned. Reserve 2 tablespoons drippings in skillet with pancetta. Discard garlic and remaining drippings.

3. Add wine to pancetta mixture; cook over medium heat 3 minutes or until wine has almost evaporated. Add cream; cook and stir 2 minutes. Remove from heat.

4. Whisk egg and egg yolk in top of double boiler. Place top of double boiler over simmering water, adjusting heat to maintain simmer. Whisk ⅓ cup cheese and pepper into egg mixture; cook and stir until sauce has thickened slightly.

5. Pour pancetta mixture over fettuccine; toss to coat. Cook over medium-low heat until heated through. Add egg mixture; toss to coat. Sprinkle with remaining ⅓ cup cheese; serve immediately.

Fettuccine alla Carbonara

Shells and Gorgonzola

Makes 4 to 6 servings

1 package (16 ounces) uncooked medium shell pasta
1 jar (24 ounces) vodka sauce
1 package (4 ounces) crumbled Gorgonzola cheese

1. Cook pasta according to package directions. Drain well; cover and keep warm.

2. Heat sauce in medium saucepan over medium heat.

3. Toss pasta with sauce until well blended. Stir in cheese just before serving.

Variation: Add 2 cups packed torn stemmed spinach to cooked pasta. Toss pasta mixture with sauce until well blended. Stir in cheese and sprinkle with chopped fresh rosemary just before serving.

TIP: Gorgonzola is a type of blue cheese from Italy. Made from cow's milk, it is rich and creamy with a distinctive aroma. If you can't find Gorgonzola cheese in your supermarket, substitute another blue cheese or any other strongly-flavored cheese.

Shells and Gorgonzola

Ham and Swiss Penne Skillet

Makes 4 servings

2 ounces bread, torn into small pieces
5 tablespoons butter, divided
4 cups water
6 ounces uncooked penne pasta
3 tablespoons all-purpose flour
2¾ cups whole milk
6 ounces ham, diced
1½ cups (6 ounces) shredded Swiss cheese
1 cup frozen corn, thawed
¾ cup frozen peas, thawed
½ cup finely chopped green onions
Salt and black pepper

1. Place bread in food processor and pulse until coarse crumbs form.

2. Melt 2 tablespoons butter in large skillet over medium heat, tilting skillet to coat evenly. Add bread crumbs; cook and stir 2 minutes or until golden brown. Transfer to plate; set aside.

3. Add water to skillet and bring to a boil over high heat. Add pasta. Return to a boil; cook until just tender, stirring occasionally. Drain well; cover and keep warm.

4. Melt remaining 3 tablespoons butter in same skillet over medium heat. Add flour; whisk until smooth. Cook and stir 2 minutes. Gradually add milk, whisking constantly until well blended. Cook and stir 4 minutes or until slightly thickened, scraping down side and bottom occasionally.

5. Add pasta, ham, cheese, corn, peas and green onions; stir gently to blend. Season with salt and pepper. Cook 4 minutes or until thickened. Remove from heat; sprinkle with bread crumbs. Serve immediately.

Ham and Swiss Penne Skillet

Mac & Mornay

Makes 6 servings

>   12 ounces uncooked elbow macaroni
>   6 tablespoons butter
>   6 tablespoons all-purpose flour
>   1 teaspoon salt
>   2 cups milk, warmed
>   ½ cup grated Romano cheese
>   Dash ground nutmeg
>   Additional grated Romano cheese (optional)

1. Cook macaroni according to package directions. Drain well; cover and keep warm.

2. Melt butter in 2-quart saucepan over medium heat. Whisk in flour and salt; cook 2 minutes. Gradually whisk in milk until well blended. Cook 3 to 4 minutes or until slightly thickened, whisking occasionally.

3. Remove from heat. Stir in cheese and nutmeg.

4. Toss macaroni with sauce. Sprinkle with additional cheese, if desired.

Southwestern Skillet Macaroni

Makes 4 servings

>   1½ cups elbow macaroni
>   1 pound ground beef
>   ¼ cup chili powder
>   1 can (28 ounces) crushed tomatoes in purée
>   ⅓ cup *Frank's® RedHot®* Original Cayenne Pepper Sauce
>   1 cup (4 ounces) shredded Cheddar cheese

1. Cook macaroni in boiling water 5 minutes. Drain.

2. In large nonstick skillet, cook ground beef with chili powder until meat is browned. Add tomatoes and *Frank's RedHot* Sauce. Heat to boiling. Reduce heat to medium. Cook 5 minutes.

3. Add macaroni; cook 5 minutes or until pasta is tender and has absorbed excess liquid. Sprinkle with cheese.

PREP TIME: 10 minutes
COOK TIME: 10 minutes

Mac & Mornay

Three-Pepper Fettuccine

Makes 4 servings

1 *each* **red bell pepper, yellow bell pepper and jalapeño pepper,***
    roasted (see Tip)
1 tablespoon olive oil
½ **teaspoon chopped fresh thyme** *or* ¼ **teaspoon dried thyme**
    Salt and black pepper
1 **package (9 ounces) refrigerated uncooked fettuccine**
1 **package (4 ounces) goat cheese crumbles**
2 **tablespoons minced chives**

*Jalapeño peppers can sting and irritate the skin, so wear rubber gloves when handling peppers and do not touch eyes.

1. Core and seed roasted bell peppers; cut into thin strips. Place in large bowl. Core, seed and mince roasted jalapeño pepper; add to bowl. Stir in oil and thyme. Season with salt and black pepper.

2. Cook fettuccine according to package directions; drain well. Add fettuccine to pepper mixture. Toss well. Add cheese; toss until blended. Sprinkle with chives.

TIP: To roast peppers, broil on foil-lined baking sheet or broiler pan, turning occasionally, until peppers are charred all over. Place peppers in medium bowl. Cover with plastic wrap; let stand 10 minutes. Remove charred skin from peppers. Proceed with recipe. If desired, peppers can be roasted in advance and refrigerated.

Three-Pepper Fettuccine

Skillet Vegetable Lasagna

Makes 4 Servings

1¾ cups **SWANSON® Vegetable Broth (Regular** *or* **Certified Organic)**
10 **uncooked oven-ready (no-boil) lasagna noodles**
 1 **can (10¾ ounces) CAMPBELL'S® Condensed Cream of Mushroom**
  Soup (Regular *or* **98% Fat Free)**
 1 **can (14.5 ounces) diced canned tomatoes, undrained**
 1 **package (10 ounces) frozen chopped spinach, thawed**
 1 **cup ricotta cheese**
 1 **cup shredded mozzarella cheese (4 ounces)**

1. Heat the broth in a 12-inch skillet over medium-high heat to a boil. Break up the noodles into pieces and add to the broth. Reduce the heat to low. Cook for about 3 minutes or until the noodles are tender but still firm.

2. Stir the soup, tomatoes and spinach into the skillet. Cook for about 5 minutes or until the mixture is hot and bubbling.

3. Remove the skillet from the heat. Spoon the ricotta cheese on top and sprinkle with the mozzarella cheese.

PREP TIME: 10 minutes
COOK TIME: 15 minutes

Skillet Vegetable Lasagna

Penne with Roasted Tomato Sauce and Mozzarella

Makes 4 servings

 1 teaspoon olive oil
 3 cloves garlic, minced
 2 cans (28 ounces each) fire-roasted diced tomatoes
 ¼ teaspoon black pepper
 8 ounces uncooked penne pasta
 ½ pound smoked turkey sausage, cut into ¼-inch-thick slices
 8 ounces mozzarella cheese, cut into ¼-inch cubes, at room
    temperature
 ¼ cup chopped fresh basil
    Salt

1. Heat oil in large saucepan over medium-high heat. Add garlic; cook and stir 2 minutes. Add tomatoes and pepper; bring to a boil. Reduce heat; cover and simmer 15 minutes. Cool slightly.

2. Cook pasta according to package directions. Drain well; cover and keep warm.

3. Place half of tomato mixture in blender or food processor; process just until smooth. Add tomato purée to pasta; toss to combine.

4. Heat small nonstick skillet over medium-high heat. Add sausage; cook and stir 3 minutes. Transfer sausage to remaining tomato mixture in saucepan. Cover; simmer over medium heat 5 minutes or until heated through.

5. Add pasta mixture to saucepan; toss to combine. Stir in cheese and basil. Season with salt. Serve immediately.

PREP TIME: 15 minutes
COOK TIME: 25 minutes

Penne with Roasted Tomato Sauce and Mozzarella

Creamy Fettuccine with Asparagus & Lima Beans

Makes 4 servings

8 ounces uncooked fettuccine
2 tablespoons butter
2 cups asparagus pieces (about 1 inch long)
1 cup frozen lima beans, thawed
¼ teaspoon black pepper
½ cup chicken or vegetable broth
1 cup half-and-half or whipping cream
1 cup grated Parmesan cheese

1. Cook fettuccine according to package directions. Drain well; cover and keep warm.

2. Melt butter in large skillet over medium-high heat. Add asparagus, lima beans and ¼ teaspoon pepper; cook and stir 3 minutes. Add broth; simmer 3 minutes. Add half-and-half; simmer 3 to 4 minutes or until vegetables are tender.

3. Add vegetable mixture and cheese to fettuccine; toss to combine. Serve immediately.

TIP: Lima beans are plump, kidney-shaped and pale green. They are an excellent source of protein, potassium and iron and can be found in your supermarket freezer case year-round.

Creamy Fettuccine with Asparagus & Lima Beans

Pesto Chicken Mac & Cheese

Makes 6 to 8 servings

4 cups milk
1 clove garlic, peeled and smashed
¼ cup (½ stick) butter
5 tablespoons all-purpose flour
8 ounces fontina cheese, shredded
2 cups (8 ounces) shredded mozzarella cheese
½ cup grated Parmesan cheese
½ cup prepared pesto sauce
    Salt and black pepper
1 package (6 ounces) baby spinach
1 package (about 16 ounces) radiatore or penne pasta, cooked
    and drained
1 pound boneless skinless chicken breasts, cooked and chopped

1. Bring milk and garlic to a boil in small saucepan. Reduce heat; keep warm. Discard garlic.

2. Melt butter in large saucepan over medium heat; whisk in flour. Cook and stir 2 minutes. Gradually add milk, whisking constantly until blended. Bring to a boil. Reduce heat; cook and stir 10 minutes or until thickened. Remove from heat.

3. Add cheeses to sauce mixture, whisking until smooth. Stir in pesto; season with salt and pepper. Toss spinach, pasta and chicken with pesto mixture until spinach wilts. Serve immediately.

Pesto Chicken Mac & Cheese

Pennsylvania Dutch Ham & Noodle Casserole

Makes 4 servings

1 tablespoon vegetable oil
2 cups cubed cooked ham (about 1 pound)
1 medium onion, chopped (about ½ cup)
1 can (10¾ ounces) CAMPBELL'S® Condensed Cream of Mushroom
    Soup (Regular *or* 98% Fat Free)
8 ounces extra-sharp Cheddar cheese, sliced
8 ounces extra-wide egg noodles (2 cups), cooked and drained

1. Heat the oil in a 4-quart saucepan over medium-high heat. Add the ham and onion and cook until the onion is tender.

2. Stir the soup into the saucepan. Reduce the heat to medium. Cook and stir for 5 minutes. Add the cheese and stir until the cheese melts. Gently stir in the noodles. Heat through, stirring often.

Easy Substitution Tip: Substitute cooked chicken or turkey for the ham.

PREP TIME: 10 minutes
COOK TIME: 15 minutes

Pennsylvania Dutch Ham & Noodle Casserole

Cheesy Chicken-Orzo Skillet

Makes 4 servings

1 tablespoon olive oil
1 teaspoon Greek seasoning
½ teaspoon grated lemon peel
½ teaspoon black pepper
1½ pounds boneless skinless chicken breasts, cut into 1-inch cubes
1¼ cups uncooked orzo pasta
1 can (about 14 ounces) chicken broth
6 ounces Greek green olives, drained
4 cloves garlic, minced
¾ cup crumbled feta cheese, plus additional for garnish
2 cups packed torn stemmed spinach

1. Heat oil in large nonstick skillet over medium heat. Add seasoning, lemon peel and pepper; cook and stir just until fragrant. Add chicken; cook and stir 4 minutes or until no longer pink. Stir in orzo, broth, olives and garlic. Bring to a boil over high heat. Reduce heat; simmer, partially covered, 15 minutes or until orzo is just tender, stirring occasionally.

2. Stir in cheese. Place spinach on top of mixture. Cover; let stand 2 to 3 minutes or until spinach wilts. Stir until blended. Sprinkle with additional cheese, if desired. Serve immediately.

Cheesy Chicken-Orzo Skillet

Classic Fettuccine Alfredo

Makes 4 servings

12 ounces uncooked fettuccine
⅔ cup whipping cream
6 tablespoons unsalted butter
½ teaspoon salt
Generous dash white pepper
Generous dash ground nutmeg
1 cup grated Parmesan cheese
2 tablespoons chopped fresh parsley

1. Cook pasta according to package directions. Drain well; cover and keep warm.

2. Heat cream and butter in large heavy skillet over medium-low heat until butter melts and mixture bubbles, stirring frequently. Cook and stir 2 minutes. Stir in salt, pepper and nutmeg. Remove from heat. Gradually stir in cheese until well blended and smooth. Return to heat briefly to completely blend cheese, if necessary. (Do not let sauce bubble or cheese will become lumpy and tough.)

3. Pour sauce over pasta. Cook and stir over low heat 2 to 3 minutes or until sauce has thickened and pasta is evenly coated. Sprinkle with parsley. Serve immediately.

Classic Fettuccine Alfredo

Tuna & Pasta Cheddar Melt

Makes 4 servings

1 can (10½ ounces) CAMPBELL'S® Condensed Chicken Broth
1 soup can water
3 cups uncooked corkscrew pasta
1 can (10¾ ounces) CAMPBELL'S® Condensed Cream of Mushroom
    Soup (Regular *or* 98% Fat Free)
1 cup milk
1 can (about 6 ounces) tuna, drained and flaked
1 cup shredded Cheddar cheese (4 ounces)
2 tablespoons Italian-seasoned dry bread crumbs
2 teaspoons butter *or* margarine, melted

1. Heat the broth and water in a 10-inch skillet over high heat to a boil. Add the pasta. Reduce the heat to medium. Cook until the pasta is tender but still firm, stirring often. Do not drain.

2. Stir the soup, milk and tuna into the skillet. Top with the cheese. Mix the bread crumbs with the butter in a small cup. Sprinkle the crumb mixture over the tuna mixture. Cook until the mixture is hot and bubbling.

PREP/COOK TIME: 20 minutes

 TIP: Canned tuna is available as either solid or chunk. Chunk tuna consists of smaller pieces and is often much less expensive than solid tuna. It is ideal for tasty casseroles like this one.

Tuna & Pasta Cheddar Melt

Baked Mac & Cheese

Layered Pasta Casserole

Makes 6 to 8 servings

8 ounces uncooked penne pasta
8 ounces mild Italian sausage, casings removed
8 ounces ground beef
1 jar (about 26 ounces) pasta sauce
2 cups (8 ounces) shredded mozzarella cheese, divided
1 package (10 ounces) frozen chopped spinach, thawed and
    squeezed dry
1 cup ricotta cheese
½ cup grated Parmesan cheese
1 egg
2 tablespoons chopped fresh basil *or* 2 teaspoons dried basil
1 teaspoon salt

1. Preheat oven to 350°F. Spray 13×9-inch baking dish with nonstick cooking spray.

2. Cook pasta according to package directions. Drain well; transfer to prepared baking dish.

3. Brown sausage and ground beef in large skillet over medium-high heat, stirring to break up meat; drain fat. Add pasta sauce; mix well. Add half of sauce mixture to pasta; toss to coat.

4. Combine 1 cup mozzarella cheese, spinach, ricotta cheese, Parmesan cheese, egg, basil and salt in medium bowl. Spoon small mounds of spinach mixture over pasta mixture; spread evenly. Top with remaining sauce mixture; sprinkle with remaining 1 cup mozzarella cheese. Bake 30 minutes or until bubbly.

Four-Cheese Mac & Cheese

Makes 8 servings

    1 package (16 ounces) uncooked elbow macaroni
    4 cups milk
    4 cups (16 ounces) shredded sharp Cheddar cheese
    4 cups (16 ounces) shredded American cheese
    2 cups (8 ounces) shredded Muenster cheese
    2 cups (8 ounces) shredded mozzarella cheese
    ½ cup bread crumbs (optional)

1. Preheat oven to 350°F. Cook macaroni according to package directions. Drain well; cover and keep warm.

2. Bring milk to a simmer in large saucepan over medium heat. Do not boil. Reduce heat to low. Gradually add cheeses, stirring constantly. Cook and stir 5 minutes or until melted.

3. Place macaroni in 4-quart casserole or individual ovenproof dishes. Pour cheese mixture over pasta; stir until well blended. Sprinkle with bread crumbs, if desired. Bake 50 to 60 minutes (25 to 30 minutes for individual dishes) or until bubbly.

Beef and Veg•All® Cheddar Bake

Makes 4 to 6 servings

    2 cups cooked elbow macaroni
    1 pound extra-lean ground beef, cooked and drained
    2 cans (15 ounces each) VEG•ALL® Original Mixed Vegetables, drained
    ½ cup chopped onion
    ¼ teaspoon black pepper
    3 cups shredded Cheddar cheese

Preheat oven to 350°F. In large mixing bowl, combine macaroni, ground beef, Veg•All, onion, pepper and cheese; mix well.

Pour mixture into large casserole dish. Bake 30 to 35 minutes. Serve hot.

Four-Cheese Mac & Cheese

Cauliflower Mac & Gouda

Makes 6 to 8 servings

> 1 package (about 16 ounces) uncooked bowtie pasta
> 4 cups milk
> 2 cloves garlic, peeled and smashed
> ¼ cup (½ stick) plus 3 tablespoons butter, divided
> 5 tablespoons all-purpose flour
> 16 ounces Gouda cheese, shredded
> 1 teaspoon ground mustard
> ⅛ teaspoon smoked paprika or regular paprika
>   Salt and black pepper
> 1 head cauliflower, cored and cut into florets
> 1 cup panko bread crumbs

1. Bring 6 quarts of water to a boil in pasta pot with insert. Add pasta; cook according to package directions or until almost tender. Drain pasta, reserving pasta water; keep warm. Return water to a boil.

2. Bring milk and garlic to a boil in small saucepan. Reduce heat; keep warm. Discard garlic.

3. Melt ¼ cup butter in large saucepan over medium heat; whisk in flour. Cook 1 minute, whisking constantly. Gradually add milk, whisking after each addition. Bring to a boil. Reduce heat; cook and stir 10 minutes or until thickened. Remove from heat.

4. Add cheese, mustard and paprika to sauce mixture; whisk occasionally until melted. Season with salt and pepper. Keep warm.

5. Preheat broiler. Add cauliflower to boiling pasta water. Cook 3 to 5 minutes or just until tender; drain. Toss pasta and cauliflower with sauce mixture. Spoon pasta mixture into 10 to 12 ramekins or 13×9-inch baking dish.

6. Melt remaining 3 tablespoons butter in small saucepan over medium heat. Add panko; stir just until moistened. Remove from heat. Sprinkle panko mixture over pasta mixture. Broil 2 minutes or until golden brown.

Cauliflower Mac & Gouda

Italian Three-Cheese Macaroni

Makes 4 servings

8 ounces uncooked elbow macaroni
¼ cup (½ stick) butter
3 tablespoons all-purpose flour
1 teaspoon Italian seasoning
½ to 1 teaspoon black pepper
½ teaspoon salt
2 cups milk
¾ cup (3 ounces) shredded Cheddar cheese
¼ cup grated Parmesan cheese
1 can (about 14 ounces) diced tomatoes, drained
1 cup (4 ounces) shredded mozzarella cheese
½ cup plain dry bread crumbs

1. Preheat oven to 350°F. Spray 2-quart round casserole with nonstick cooking spray.

2. Cook macaroni according to package directions. Drain well; cover and keep warm.

3. Melt butter in medium saucepan over medium heat. Whisk in flour, seasoning, pepper and salt until smooth. Cook and stir 2 minutes. Gradually add milk, whisking constantly until slightly thickened. Add Cheddar and Parmesan cheeses; stir until smooth.

4. Layer half of pasta, half of tomatoes and half of cheese sauce in prepared casserole. Repeat layers.

5. Sprinkle mozzarella cheese evenly over casserole. Place bread crumbs in small bowl; spray several times with cooking spray. Sprinkle over casserole.

6. Cover; bake 30 minutes or until bubbly. Uncover; bake 5 minutes or until golden brown.

Chicken Tetrazzini

Makes 6 servings

½ cup chopped onion
½ cup chopped celery
¼ cup (½ stick) butter or margarine
1 can (13¾ ounces) chicken broth
1 package (8 ounces) PHILADELPHIA® Cream Cheese, cubed
¾ cup KRAFT® 100% Grated Parmesan Cheese, divided
1 package (7 ounces) spaghetti, cooked, drained
1 jar (6 ounces) whole mushrooms, drained
1 cup chopped cooked chicken or turkey

COOK and stir onion and celery in butter in large skillet on medium heat until tender. Add broth, cream cheese and ½ cup of the Parmesan cheese; cook on low heat until cream cheese is melted, stirring occasionally.

ADD all remaining ingredients except remaining Parmesan cheese; mix lightly. Spoon into 12×8-inch baking dish; sprinkle with remaining ¼ cup Parmesan cheese.

BAKE at 350°F for 30 minutes.

PREP TIME: 20 minutes
BAKE TIME: 30 minutes

Cheesy Tuna Noodle Casserole

Makes 4 servings

**1 can (10¾ ounces) CAMPBELL'S® Condensed Cream of Mushroom
    Soup (Regular *or* 98% Fat Free)**
½ cup milk
1 cup frozen peas
2 cans (about 6 ounces each) tuna, drained and flaked
2 cups hot cooked medium egg noodles
½ cup shredded Cheddar cheese

1. Stir the soup, milk, peas, tuna and noodles in a 1½-quart casserole.

2. Bake at 400°F. for 20 minutes or until hot. Stir.

3. Sprinkle cheese over the tuna mixture. Bake for 2 minutes more or until
the cheese melts.

Easy Substitution Tip: Substitute your family's favorite frozen vegetable
for the peas.

PREP TIME: 10 minutes
BAKE TIME: 22 minutes

Cheesy Tuna Noodle Casserole

Three-Cheese Baked Ziti with Spinach

1 box (16 ounces) medium tube-shaped pasta (ziti)
1 bag (6 ounces) baby spinach leaves (4 cups), washed
1 jar (1 pound 9 ounces) PREGO® Marinara Italian Sauce
1 cup ricotta cheese
1 cup shredded mozzarella cheese (4 ounces)
¾ cup grated Parmesan cheese
½ teaspoon garlic powder
¼ teaspoon ground black pepper

1. Prepare the pasta according to the package directions. Add the spinach during the last minute of the cooking time. Drain the pasta and spinach well in a colander. Return them to the saucepot.

2. Stir the Italian sauce, ricotta, ½ **cup** of the mozzarella cheese, ½ **cup** of the Parmesan cheese, garlic powder and black pepper into the pasta mixture. Spoon the pasta mixture into a 13×9×2-inch shallow baking dish. Sprinkle with the remaining mozzarella and Parmesan cheeses.

3. Bake at 350°F. for 30 minutes or until hot and bubbly.

Make Ahead: Prepare through step 2. Cover and refrigerate up to 6 hours. Uncover and let come to room temperature before baking.

PREP TIME: 15 minutes
BAKE TIME: 30 minutes

Three-Cheese Baked Ziti with Spinach

Veggie Mac & Cheese

Makes 4 servings

6 ounces uncooked elbow macaroni, rotini or penne pasta
2 tablespoons all-purpose flour
1¼ cups milk, divided
1 cup (4 ounces) shredded sharp Cheddar cheese
½ cup shredded Parmesan cheese
1½ cups frozen mixed vegetables, cooked and drained
Salt and black pepper

1. Preheat oven to 325°F. Coat 1½-quart baking dish with nonstick cooking spray.

2. Cook macaroni according to package directions. Drain well; cover and keep warm.

3. Stir together flour and ¼ cup milk in small saucepan until smooth. Add remaining milk; mix until smooth. Simmer over medium heat until thickened, stirring constantly.

4. Combine cheeses in medium bowl. Add half of cheese mixture to milk mixture; stir until smooth. Stir in macaroni and vegetables. Season with salt and pepper.

5. Spoon macaroni mixture into prepared baking dish. Sprinkle with remaining half of cheese mixture. Bake 20 minutes or until bubbly. Let stand 15 minutes before serving.

Veggie Mac & Cheese

Creamy 3-Cheese Pasta

Makes 4 servings

**1 can (10¾ ounces) CAMPBELL'S® Condensed Cream of Mushroom
Soup (Regular *or* 98% Fat Free)**
1 cup milk
¼ teaspoon ground black pepper
1 package (8 ounces) shredded two-cheese blend
⅓ cup grated Parmesan cheese
3 cups corkscrew-shaped pasta (rotelle), cooked and drained

1. Stir the soup, milk, black pepper and cheeses in a 1½-quart casserole
dish. Stir in the pasta.

2. Bake at 400°F. for 20 minutes or until hot.

3. Stir before serving.

PREP/BAKE TIME: 25 minutes

 TIP: If you can't find the corkscrew-shaped pasta
called for in the recipe, you can substitute penne
pasta or any other small shape.

Creamy 3-Cheese Pasta

Broccoli Mac & Cheese

8 ounces uncooked elbow macaroni
¼ cup (½ stick) butter
¼ cup all-purpose flour
2 cups milk
8 ounces sharp Cheddar cheese, cubed
2 ounces pepper jack cheese, cubed (optional)
½ cup chopped onion
2 cups (about 16 ounces) broccoli florets, cooked and drained
2 English muffins, cut into ½-inch pieces

1. Preheat oven to 350°F.

2. Cook macaroni according to package directions. Drain well; transfer to 3-quart casserole.

3. Melt butter in large saucepan over medium heat. Whisk in flour until smooth. Cook and stir 2 minutes. Gradually add milk, whisking constantly until blended. Cook and stir 3 to 4 minutes or thickened.

4. Add Cheddar cheese, pepper jack cheese, if desired, and onion to milk mixture. Cook 2 minutes or until cheese melts, whisking constantly. Add broccoli; stir well.

5. Pour cheese mixture over macaroni; mix well. Sprinkle English muffin pieces evenly over top. Bake 15 to 20 minutes or until muffin pieces are golden brown.

Chicken Asparagus Gratin

Makes 4 servings

> 1 can (10¾ ounces) CAMPBELL'S® Condensed Cream of Asparagus
>   Soup
> ½ cup milk
> ¼ teaspoon onion powder
> ⅛ teaspoon black pepper
> 1½ cups cooked cut asparagus
> 1½ cups cubed cooked chicken
>   3 cups corkscrew-shaped pasta (rotelle), cooked and drained
>   1 cup shredded Cheddar or Swiss cheese (4 ounces)

1. Stir the soup, milk, onion powder, black pepper, asparagus, chicken, pasta and ½ **cup** of the cheese in a 12×8×2-inch shallow baking dish.

2. Bake at 400°F. for 25 minutes or until hot. Stir.

3. Sprinkle with the remaining cheese. Bake for 5 minutes more or until cheese melts.

PREP TIME: 20 minutes
BAKE TIME: 30 minutes

TIP: For 1½ cups cooked cut asparagus, cook ¾ pound fresh asparagus, trimmed and cut into 1-inch pieces, or 1 package (about 9 ounces) frozen asparagus cuts.

3-Cheese Baked Ham and Tortellini

Makes 4 to 6 servings

2 tablespoons minced onion
2 cloves garlic, minced
1½ tablespoons butter or margarine
2 tablespoons all-purpose flour
1½ cups milk
¼ cup shredded mozzarella cheese
¼ cup shredded Parmesan cheese
¼ cup shredded Swiss cheese
1 cup (6 ounces) finely chopped **HORMEL® CURE 81®** ham
¼ teaspoon white pepper
4 cups cooked cheese-filled tortellini
Chopped fresh parsley

In small saucepan over medium-low heat, cook onion and garlic in butter until tender. Stir in flour. Cook 2 minutes, stirring constantly. Gradually stir in milk. Simmer 10 to 15 minutes or until thickened, stirring frequently. Add cheeses. Stir until melted. Stir in ham and white pepper. Spoon pasta into 4 to 6 individual gratin dishes. Spoon sauce over pasta. Broil 4 inches from heat source 3 to 5 minutes or until topping is slightly golden. Sprinkle with chopped parsley.

3-Cheese Baked Ham and Tortellini

Baked Rigatoni

Makes 8 servings

1 pound dry rigatoni
4 ounces mild Italian sausage, casings removed, sliced
1 cup chopped onion
2 cloves garlic, minced
1 can (14.5 ounces) CONTADINA® Recipe Ready Diced Tomatoes, undrained
1 can (6 ounces) CONTADINA Tomato Paste
1 cup chicken broth
1 teaspoon salt
1 cup (4 ounces) shredded mozzarella cheese, divided
½ cup (2 ounces) shredded Parmesan cheese (optional)
2 tablespoons chopped fresh basil or 2 teaspoons dried basil leaves, crushed

1. Cook pasta according to package directions. Drain and keep warm.

2. Meanwhile, cook sausage in large skillet for 4 to 6 minutes or until no longer pink. Remove sausage from skillet, reserving any drippings in skillet.

3. Add onion and garlic to skillet; sauté for 2 minutes. Stir in undrained tomatoes, tomato paste, broth and salt.

4. Bring to a boil. Reduce heat to low; simmer, uncovered, for 10 minutes, stirring occasionally.

5. Combine pasta, tomato mixture, sausage, ½ cup mozzarella cheese, Parmesan cheese and basil in large bowl; spoon into ungreased 13×9-inch baking dish. Sprinkle with remaining mozzarella cheese.

6. Bake in preheated 375°F oven for 10 to 15 minutes or until cheese is melted.

PREP TIME: 10 minutes
COOK TIME: 33 minutes

Baked Rigatoni

Cheesy Artichoke-Chicken Rotini

Makes 6 servings

8 ounces uncooked rotini pasta
1 tablespoon olive oil
1 medium onion, chopped
½ green bell pepper, chopped
2 cups shredded cooked chicken
1 can (about 14 ounces) diced tomatoes with Italian herbs
1 can (14 ounces) artichoke hearts, drained and quartered
1 can (6 ounces) sliced black olives, drained
1 teaspoon Italian seasoning
3 cups (12 ounces) shredded mozzarella cheese

1. Preheat oven to 350°F. Spray 2-quart casserole with nonstick cooking spray.

2. Cook pasta according to package directions. Drain well; cover and keep warm.

3. Heat oil in large deep skillet over medium heat. Add onion and bell pepper; cook and stir 1 minute. Add pasta, chicken, tomatoes, artichokes, olives and seasoning; toss until blended.

4. Place half of pasta mixture in prepared casserole; sprinkle with half of cheese. Repeat layers.

5. Cover and bake 35 minutes or until hot and bubbly.

Cheesy Artichoke-Chicken Rotini

Country Sausage Macaroni and Cheese

Makes 6 to 8 servings

    1 pound **BOB EVANS®** Special Seasonings Roll Sausage
 1½ cups milk
  12 ounces pasteurized processed Cheddar cheese, cut into cubes
   ½ cup Dijon mustard
    1 cup diced fresh or drained canned tomatoes
    1 cup sliced mushrooms
   ⅓ cup sliced green onions
   ⅛ teaspoon cayenne pepper
  12 ounces uncooked elbow macaroni
    2 tablespoons grated Parmesan cheese

Preheat oven to 350°F. Crumble and cook sausage in medium skillet until browned. Drain on paper towels. Combine milk, processed cheese and mustard in medium saucepan; cook and stir over low heat until cheese melts and mixture is smooth. Stir in sausage, tomatoes, mushrooms, green onions and cayenne pepper. Remove from heat.

Cook macaroni according to package directions; drain. Combine hot macaroni and cheese mixture in large bowl; toss until well coated. Spoon into greased shallow 2-quart casserole dish. Cover and bake 15 to 20 minutes. Stir; sprinkle with Parmesan cheese. Bake, uncovered, 5 minutes more. Let stand 10 minutes before serving. Refrigerate leftovers.

Spinach-Cheese Pasta Bake

Makes 6 to 8 servings

8 ounces uncooked shell pasta
2 eggs
1 package (10 ounces) frozen chopped spinach, thawed and
squeezed dry
1 cup ricotta cheese
1 jar (26 ounces) marinara sauce
1 teaspoon salt
2 cups (8 ounces) shredded mozzarella cheese
¼ cup grated Parmesan cheese

1. Preheat oven to 350°F. Spray 1½-quart round casserole with nonstick cooking spray.

2. Cook pasta according to package directions. Drain well; cover and keep warm.

3. Whisk eggs in large bowl until blended. Add spinach and ricotta cheese; stir until blended. Stir in pasta, marinara sauce and salt until pasta is well coated. Transfer to prepared casserole. Sprinkle with mozzarella and Parmesan cheeses.

4. Cover; bake 30 minutes. Uncover; bake 15 minutes or until bubbly.

Baked Pasta with Ricotta

Makes 12 servings

1 package (16 ounces) uncooked rigatoni or penne pasta
1 container (15 ounces) ricotta cheese
⅔ cup grated Parmesan cheese
2 eggs, lightly beaten
½ teaspoon salt
⅛ teaspoon black pepper
2 jars (26 ounces each) marinara sauce, divided
3 cups (12 ounces) shredded mozzarella cheese, divided

1. Preheat oven to 375°F. Spray 13×9-inch baking dish with nonstick cooking spray.

2. Cook pasta according to package directions. Drain well; cover and keep warm.

3. Combine ricotta cheese, Parmesan cheese, eggs, salt and pepper in medium bowl until well blended.

4. Spread 2 cups marinara sauce over bottom of prepared dish; spoon half of pasta over sauce. Top with half of ricotta mixture and 1 cup mozzarella cheese. Repeat layers. Top with remaining marinara sauce and 1 cup mozzarella cheese.

5. Cover with foil; bake 1 hour or until bubbly. Uncover; bake 5 minutes or until cheese begins to brown at edges. Let stand 15 minutes before serving.

Baked Pasta with Ricotta

Creamy Confetti Macaroni

Makes 6 servings

8 ounces uncooked elbow macaroni
1 cup chopped onion
1 cup chopped red or green bell pepper
¾ cup chopped celery
1 cup cottage cheese
1 cup (4 ounces) shredded Swiss cheese
½ cup (2 ounces) shredded American cheese
½ cup milk
3 egg whites
3 tablespoons all-purpose flour
1 tablespoon butter
¼ teaspoon black pepper
¼ teaspoon hot pepper sauce

1. Preheat oven to 350°F. Coat 2-quart casserole with nonstick cooking spray.

2. Cook macaroni according to package directions. Add onion, bell pepper and celery during last 5 minutes of cooking. Drain pasta and vegetables well; cover and keep warm.

3. Combine cottage cheese, Swiss cheese, American cheese, milk, egg whites, flour, butter, black pepper and pepper sauce in food processor or blender. Process until smooth. Stir cheese mixture into pasta and vegetables.

4. Spoon mixture into prepared casserole. Bake 35 to 40 minutes or until bubbly. Let stand 15 minutes before serving.

Creamy Confetti Macaroni

Macaroni & Cheese with Bacon

Makes 4 servings

3 cups (8 ounces) uncooked rotini pasta
2 tablespoons butter
2 tablespoons all-purpose flour
¼ teaspoon salt
¼ teaspoon ground mustard
⅛ teaspoon black pepper
1½ cups milk
2 cups (8 ounces) shredded sharp Cheddar cheese
8 ounces bacon, crisp-cooked and crumbled
2 medium tomatoes, sliced

1. Preheat oven to 350°F. Lightly grease shallow 1½-quart casserole.

2. Cook pasta according to package directions. Drain well; cover and keep warm.

3. Melt butter in medium saucepan over medium-low heat. Whisk in flour, salt, mustard and pepper until smooth. Cook and stir 2 minutes. Gradually add milk, whisking constantly until well blended. Cook and stir 3 to 4 minutes or until thickened. Remove from heat. Add cheese; stir until melted.

4. Toss pasta with cheese mixture and bacon until well blended. Transfer to prepared casserole. Bake 20 minutes. Arrange tomato slices on top of casserole. Bake 5 to 8 minutes or until casserole is bubbly and tomatoes are heated through.

Macaroni & Cheese with Bacon

Baked Macaroni & Cheese

Makes 4 servings

1 can (10¾ ounces) CAMPBELL'S® Condensed Cheddar Cheese Soup
½ soup can milk
⅛ teaspoon pepper
2 cups hot cooked corkscrew *or* medium shell macaroni (about
**   1½ cups uncooked)**
1 tablespoon dry bread crumbs
2 teaspoons butter, melted

1. Stir the soup, milk, black pepper and pasta in a 1-quart casserole.

2. Mix the bread crumbs with the butter in a small bowl. Sprinkle over the pasta mixture.

3. Bake at 400°F. for 20 minutes or until hot.

To Double Recipe: Double all ingredients, except increase butter to 1 tablespoon, use 2-quart casserole and increase baking time to 25 minutes.

Variation: Substitute 2 cups hot cooked elbow macaroni (about 1 cup uncooked) for corkscrew *or* shell macaroni.

PREP TIME: 20 minutes
BAKE TIME: 20 minutes

Enlightened Macaroni and Cheese

Makes 4 servings

8 ounces uncooked wagon wheel, bowtie or elbow pasta
1 tablespoon all-purpose flour
2 teaspoons cornstarch
¼ teaspoon ground mustard
1 can (12 ounces) evaporated milk
1 cup (4 ounces) shredded sharp Cheddar cheese
½ cup (2 ounces) shredded Monterey Jack cheese
1 jar (2 ounces) diced pimiento, drained
1 teaspoon Worcestershire sauce
¼ teaspoon black pepper
1 tablespoon plain dry bread crumbs
1 tablespoon paprika

1. Preheat oven to 375°F. Spray 1½-quart casserole with nonstick cooking spray.

2. Cook pasta according to package directions. Drain well; cover and keep warm.

3. Combine flour, cornstarch and mustard in medium saucepan; stir in evaporated milk until smooth. Cook and stir over low heat 8 minutes or until slightly thickened.

4. Remove from heat; stir in cheeses, pimiento, Worcestershire sauce and pepper. Add pasta; mix well.

5. Spoon mixture into prepared casserole; sprinkle with bread crumbs and paprika. Bake 20 minutes or until bubbly and heated through.

Fancy Mac & Cheese

Southwestern Corn and Pasta Casserole

 2 tablespoons vegetable oil
 1 red bell pepper, chopped
 1 onion, chopped
 1 jalapeño pepper,* minced
 1 clove garlic, minced
 1 cup sliced mushrooms
 2 cups frozen corn
 ½ teaspoon salt
 ¼ teaspoon ground cumin
 ¼ teaspoon chili powder
 4 ounces whole wheat elbow macaroni, cooked and drained
1½ cups milk
 1 tablespoon unsalted butter
 1 tablespoon all-purpose flour
 2 cups (8 ounces) shredded pepper jack cheese
 1 slice whole wheat bread, cut or torn into ½-inch pieces

Jalapeño peppers can sting and irritate the skin, so wear rubber gloves when handling peppers and do not touch your eyes.

1. Preheat oven to 350°F. Grease 3-quart baking dish.

2. Heat oil in large skillet over medium-high heat. Add bell pepper, onion, jalapeño pepper and garlic; cook and stir 5 minutes. Add mushrooms; cook and stir 5 minutes. Add corn, salt, cumin and chili powder. Reduce heat to low; cook 5 minutes or until corn thaws. Stir in macaroni; set aside.

3. Bring milk to a simmer in small saucepan over low heat. Melt butter in large saucepan over medium heat. Whisk in flour until smooth. Cook and stir 2 minutes. Gradually add milk, whisking constantly until well blended. Cook and stir 3 to 4 minutes or until thickened. Gradually stir in cheese. Cook and stir over low heat until cheese melts. Stir macaroni mixture into cheese sauce; mix well.

4. Spoon into prepared baking dish. Sprinkle bread pieces over casserole. Bake 20 to 25 minutes or until bubbly. Let stand 15 minutes before serving.

Broccoli and Pasta Bianco

Makes 8 servings

1 package (16 ounces) medium tube-shaped pasta (penne)
4 cups fresh or frozen broccoli flowerets
1 can (10¾ ounces) CAMPBELL'S® Condensed Cream of Mushroom
    Soup (Regular *or* 98% Fat Free)
1½ cups milk
½ teaspoon ground black pepper
1½ cups shredded mozzarella cheese (6 ounces)
¼ cup shredded Parmesan cheese

1. Prepare the pasta according to the package directions. Add the broccoli during the last 4 minutes of the cooking time. Drain the pasta and broccoli well in a colander.

2. Stir together the soup, milk and black pepper in a 12×8×2-inch shallow baking dish. Stir in the pasta mixture, ¾ **cup** of the mozzarella cheese and **2 tablespoons** of the Parmesan cheese. Top with the remaining mozzarella and Parmesan cheeses.

3. Bake at 350°F. for 25 minutes or until hot and the cheese melts.

PREP TIME: 20 minutes
BAKE TIME: 25 minutes

Broccoli and Pasta Bianco

No-Chop Pastitsio

Makes 6 servings

1 pound ground beef or ground lamb
1½ cups mild picante sauce
1 can (8 ounces) tomato sauce
1 tablespoon sugar
½ teaspoon ground allspice
½ teaspoon ground cinnamon
¼ teaspoon ground nutmeg, divided
8 ounces uncooked elbow macaroni
3 tablespoons butter
3 tablespoons all-purpose flour
1½ cups milk
½ teaspoon salt
¼ teaspoon black pepper
2 eggs, beaten
½ cup grated Parmesan cheese

1. Preheat oven to 350°F. Lightly spray 9-inch square baking dish with nonstick cooking spray.

2. For meat sauce, brown beef in large skillet over medium-high heat, stirring to break up meat; drain fat. Add picante sauce, tomato sauce, sugar, allspice, cinnamon and ⅛ teaspoon nutmeg. Bring to a boil; reduce heat and simmer, uncovered, 10 minutes, stirring frequently.

3. Cook macaroni according to package directions. Drain well; transfer to prepared baking dish.

4. For white sauce, melt butter in medium saucepan over medium heat. Whisk in flour until smooth. Cook and stir 2 minutes. Gradually add milk, whisking constantly until well blended. Cook and stir 3 to 4 minutes or until thickened. Remove from heat. Add about ½ cup white sauce to eggs; stir to blend thoroughly. Add egg mixture to remaining white sauce in saucepan. Stir in Parmesan cheese.

5. Stir about ½ cup white sauce into macaroni until coated. Spread meat sauce over macaroni. Top with remaining white sauce. Sprinkle with remaining ⅛ teaspoon nutmeg. Bake 30 to 40 minutes or until knife inserted into center comes out clean. Let stand 15 minutes before serving.

No-Chop Pastitsio

Spicy Jac Mac & Cheese with Broccoli

Makes 8 servings

2 cups (8 ounces) dry elbow macaroni
2 cups chopped frozen or fresh broccoli
2 cups (8 ounces) shredded sharp Cheddar cheese
2 cups (8 ounces) shredded pepper jack cheese
1 can (12 fluid ounces) NESTLÉ® CARNATION® Evaporated Milk
½ cup grated Parmesan cheese, divided
½ teaspoon ground black pepper
2 tablespoons bread crumbs

Preheat oven to 350°F. Lightly butter 2½-quart casserole dish.

Cook macaroni in large saucepan according to package directions, adding broccoli to boiling pasta water for last 3 minutes of cooking time; drain.

Combine cooked pasta, broccoli, Cheddar cheese, pepper jack cheese, evaporated milk, ¼ cup Parmesan cheese and black pepper in large bowl. Pour into prepared casserole dish. Combine remaining Parmesan cheese and bread crumbs; sprinkle over macaroni mixture. Cover tightly with aluminum foil.

Bake covered for 20 minutes. Remove foil; bake for additional 10 minutes or until lightly browned.

TIP: For a less spicy version, substitute 2 cups (8 ounces) shredded Monterey Jack cheese and a few dashes of hot pepper sauce, if desired, for the pepper jack cheese.

Creamy Fettuccine with Prosciutto and Peas

Makes 2 to 4 servings

8 ounces uncooked fettuccine
2 tablespoons olive oil
4 cloves garlic, minced
3 ounces thinly sliced prosciutto or salami, cut into thin strips
1 cup frozen baby peas, thawed
1 cup half-and-half or whipping cream
½ teaspoon salt
½ teaspoon black pepper
1 cup grated Parmesan cheese
Julienned fresh basil (optional)

1. Cook fettuccine according to package directions. Drain well; cover and keep warm.

2. Heat oil in large skillet over medium heat. Add garlic; cook and stir 2 minutes. Add prosciutto and peas; cook and stir 2 minutes. Stir in half-and-half, salt and pepper; cook and stir 3 minutes.

3. Add fettuccine to skillet; stir to coat. Stir in cheese. Sprinkle with basil, if desired. Serve immediately.

Not Your Gramma's Kugel

Makes 6 servings

    Vegetable cooking spray
1 package (12 ounces) uncooked medium egg noodles
½ cup currants
1 can (10¾ ounces) CAMPBELL'S® Condensed Cheddar Cheese Soup
1 cup small curd cottage cheese
¾ cup sugar
1 teaspoon grated orange peel
2 eggs, beaten

SLOW COOKER DIRECTIONS

1. Spray inside of 3½-quart slow cooker with cooking spray.

2. Cook the noodles according to package directions until almost done. Drain and place in the slow cooker. Sprinkle with the currants.

3. Beat the soup, cottage cheese, sugar, orange peel and eggs with a fork in a medium bowl. Pour over the noodles. Stir to coat.

4. Cover and cook on LOW 2 to 2½ hours or until set. Serve warm.

Note: For a tasty breakfast, reheat leftover kugel in the microwave.

PREP TIME: 10 minutes
COOK TIME: 2 to 2½ hours

TIP: Kugel is a traditional Jewish casserole made with noodles or potatoes. Extra ingredients can turn it savory or sweet. This slow cooker version is perfect for potlucks or as an easy brunch dish.

Not Your Gramma's Kugel

Pizza Casserole

Makes 6 servings

8 ounces uncooked rotini or other spiral pasta
1½ to 2 pounds ground beef
1 medium onion, chopped
    Salt and black pepper
1 can (about 15 ounces) pizza sauce
1 can (8 ounces) tomato sauce
1 can (6 ounces) tomato paste
½ teaspoon sugar
½ teaspoon garlic salt
½ teaspoon dried oregano
2 cups (8 ounces) shredded mozzarella cheese
12 to 15 slices pepperoni

1. Preheat oven to 350°F. Cook pasta according to package directions; drain well and keep warm.

2. Brown beef and onion in large skillet over medium-high heat, stirring to break up meat; drain fat. Season with salt and pepper.

3. Combine pasta, pizza sauce, tomato sauce, tomato paste, sugar, garlic salt and oregano in large bowl. Add beef mixture; stir until blended.

4. Place half of mixture in 3-quart casserole or ovenproof skillet; top with 1 cup cheese. Repeat layers. Arrange pepperoni slices on top. Bake 25 to 30 minutes or until heated through and cheese is melted.

Pizza Casserole

Pasta & White Bean Casserole

Makes 6 servings

> 1 tablespoon olive oil
> ½ cup chopped onion
> 2 cloves garlic, minced
> 2 cans (about 15 ounces each) cannellini beans, rinsed and drained
> 12 ounces small shell pasta, cooked and drained
> 1 can (8 ounces) tomato sauce
> 1½ teaspoons Italian seasoning
> ½ teaspoon salt
> ½ teaspoon black pepper
> 2 cups (8 ounces) shredded Italian cheese blend
> 2 tablespoons finely chopped fresh parsley

1. Preheat oven to 350°F. Spray 2-quart casserole with nonstick cooking spray.

2. Heat oil in large skillet over medium-high heat. Add onion and garlic; cook and stir 3 to 4 minutes or until onion is tender.

3. Add beans, pasta, tomato sauce, seasoning, salt and pepper; mix well.

4. Transfer to prepared casserole; sprinkle with cheese and parsley. Bake 20 minutes or until cheese is melted.

Pasta & White Bean Casserole

Rigatoni with Four Cheeses

Makes 6 servings

3 cups milk
1 tablespoon chopped carrot
1 tablespoon chopped celery
1 tablespoon chopped onion
1 tablespoon fresh parsley sprigs
¼ teaspoon black pepper
¼ teaspoon hot pepper sauce
½ bay leaf
   Dash nutmeg
¼ cup Wisconsin butter
¼ cup flour
½ cup (2 ounces) grated Wisconsin Parmesan cheese
¼ cup (1 ounce) grated Wisconsin Romano cheese
12 ounces rigatoni, cooked, drained
1½ cups (6 ounces) shredded Wisconsin Cheddar cheese
1½ cups (6 ounces) shredded Wisconsin Mozzarella cheese
¼ teaspoon chili powder

In a 2-quart saucepan, combine milk, carrot, celery, onion, parsley, black pepper, hot pepper sauce, bay leaf and nutmeg. Bring to boil. Reduce heat to low; simmer 10 minutes. Strain, reserving liquid. Melt butter in 2-quart saucepan over low heat. Blend in flour. Gradually add reserved liquid; cook, stirring constantly, until thickened. Remove from heat. Add Parmesan and Romano cheeses; stir until blended. Pour over pasta; toss well. Combine Cheddar and Mozzarella cheese. In buttered 2-quart casserole, layer ½ of pasta mixture, Cheddar cheese mixture and remaining pasta mixture. Sprinkle with chili powder. Bake at 350°F for 25 minutes or until hot.

Favorite recipe from *Wisconsin Milk Marketing Board*

Triple Cheese & Turkey Tetrazzini

Makes 12 servings

1 (12-ounce) package extra broad egg noodles
2 (10¾-ounce) cans cheddar cheese condensed soup
1½ cups skim milk
4 teaspoons HERB-OX® chicken flavored bouillon, divided
3 cups diced cooked turkey breast
1 medium onion, chopped
1½ cups sourdough cheese-flavored croutons, crushed
3 tablespoons butter, melted
1½ cups finely shredded Monterey Jack and Cheddar cheeses

Preheat oven to 350°F. Prepare noodles as package directs. Meanwhile, in saucepan, combine soup, milk and 3 teaspoons bouillon; heat over medium heat until warmed through. In large bowl, combine prepared egg noodles, turkey, onion and soup mixture. Stir to combine ingredients thoroughly. Place turkey mixture into a 13×9-inch baking dish lightly sprayed with nonstick cooking spray. In small bowl, toss crushed croutons with melted butter and remaining bouillon. Sprinkle cheese over noodles and top with crouton mixture. Bake 40 to 45 minutes or until warmed through and golden brown.

Chile-Cheese Rotini

Makes 4 servings

5 cups cooked rotini pasta
2 cups (8 ounces) cubed American cheese
1 can (12 ounces) evaporated milk
1 cup (4 ounces) cubed sharp Cheddar cheese
1 can (4 ounces) diced green chiles, drained
2 teaspoons chili powder
2 medium tomatoes, seeded and chopped
5 green onions, thinly sliced

SLOW COOKER DIRECTIONS

1. Combine pasta, American cheese, evaporated milk, Cheddar cheese, chiles and chili powder in slow cooker; mix well. Cover; cook on HIGH 2 hours, stirring occasionally.

2. Stir in tomatoes and green onions; continue cooking until heated through.

PREP TIME: 15 minutes
COOK TIME: about 2 hours

Chile-Cheese Rotini

Tuscan Baked Rigatoni

Makes 6 to 8 servings

1 pound bulk Italian sausage
1 package (16 ounces) rigatoni pasta, cooked and drained
2 cups (8 ounces) shredded fontina cheese
2 tablespoons olive oil
2 bulbs fennel, thinly sliced
4 cloves garlic, minced
1 can (28 ounces) crushed tomatoes
1 cup whipping cream
1 teaspoon salt
1 teaspoon black pepper
8 cups packed torn stemmed spinach
1 can (about 15 ounces) cannellini beans, rinsed and drained
2 tablespoons pine nuts
½ cup grated Parmesan cheese

1. Preheat oven to 350°F. Coat 4-quart casserole with nonstick cooking spray.

2. Brown sausage in large skillet over medium-high heat, stirring to break up meat; drain fat. Transfer sausage to large bowl. Add pasta and fontina cheese; mix well.

3. Heat oil in same skillet; add fennel and garlic. Cook and stir over medium heat 3 minutes or until fennel is tender. Add tomatoes, cream, salt and pepper; cook and stir until slightly thickened. Stir in spinach, beans and pine nuts; cook until heated through.

4. Pour sauce mixture over pasta mixture; toss to coat. Transfer to prepared casserole; sprinkle evenly with Parmesan cheese. Bake 30 minutes or until bubbly.

Tuscan Baked Rigatoni

Beefy Cheddar Rotini

Makes 4 servings

2 cups broccoli florets *or* 1 package (10 ounces) frozen broccoli, thawed
1 onion, thinly sliced
½ teaspoon dried basil
½ teaspoon dried oregano
½ teaspoon dried thyme
1 can (about 14 ounces) diced tomatoes with Italian herbs
¾ cup canned beef broth
1 pound ground beef
2 cloves garlic, minced
2 cups cooked rotini pasta
1½ cups (6 ounces) shredded Cheddar cheese
2 tablespoons tomato paste

SLOW COOKER DIRECTIONS

1. Layer broccoli, onion, basil, oregano, thyme, tomatoes and broth in slow cooker. Cover; cook on LOW 2½ hours.

2. Brown beef and garlic in large nonstick skillet over medium-high heat, stirring to break up meat; drain fat. Transfer beef mixture to slow cooker. Cover; cook on LOW 2 hours.

3. Stir in pasta, cheese and tomato paste. Cover; cook on LOW 30 minutes or until cheese melts and mixture is heated through. Sprinkle with additional cheese, if desired.

Serving Suggestion: Serve with garlic bread.

Beefy Cheddar Rotini

Fettuccine with Gorgonzola Sauce

Makes 4 servings

8 ounces uncooked fettuccine
3 tablespoons butter
¼ cup all-purpose flour
2 cups milk
¼ cup canned vegetable broth
½ teaspoon black pepper
4 ounces Gorgonzola cheese, crumbled
2 teaspoons olive oil
½ pound asparagus, cut into 1-inch pieces
1 leek, cut into ½-inch pieces
1 red bell pepper, cut into short strips
2 cloves garlic, minced
1 can (15 ounces) artichoke hearts, drained and quartered
1 cup cherry tomato halves
¼ cup grated Parmesan cheese or crumbled Gorgonzola

1. Cook fettuccine according to package directions. Drain well; cover and keep warm.

2. Melt butter in small saucepan over medium heat. Whisk in flour until smooth. Cook and stir 2 to 3 minutes. Gradually stir in milk, broth and black pepper, whisking constantly until blended. Cook 3 to 4 minutes or until thickened, whisking constantly. Reduce heat to low. Stir in Gorgonzola cheese until melted.

3. Heat oil in large skillet over medium heat. Add asparagus, leek, bell pepper and garlic; cook and stir 5 to 7 minutes or until asparagus is crisp-tender. Add artichoke hearts and tomatoes; cook 2 to 3 minutes or until heated through. Add fettuccine and cheese sauce; toss to combine. Sprinkle with Parmesan cheese.

Linguine with Chipotle Cheddar and Red Peppers

Makes 6 servings

3 tablespoons olive oil
1½ large red onions, thinly sliced
2 bell peppers, thinly sliced
¼ cup dry sherry
1 jar (12 ounces) roasted red peppers, drained, thinly sliced
2 cloves garlic, minced
1 pound linguine
¼ cup chopped fresh parsley
2 tablespoons balsamic vinegar
1¾ cups (7 ounces) SARGENTO® Bistro® Blends Shredded Chipotle Cheddar Cheese, divided

1. Heat olive oil in a large nonstick skillet over high heat. Add onions and bell peppers; cook, stirring frequently, until onions are soft and beginning to brown, about 15 minutes. Stir in sherry, roasted red peppers and garlic. Simmer until liquid evaporates, about 6 minutes.

2. Cook linguine according to package directions. Drain linguine, reserving ¼ cup cooking liquid. Return linguine to pot. Add pepper mixture, parsley, vinegar, 1 cup cheese and reserved ¼ cup cooking liquid; toss well. Season to taste with salt and pepper. Divide among bowls. Top with remaining cheese.

Baked Fusilli with Roasted Vegetables

Makes 6 to 8 servings

- 1 large eggplant, cut in half
- 3 medium red bell peppers, cut in half
- 1 large sweet onion, cut into quarters
- 2 tablespoons olive oil
- 1 container (15 ounces) ricotta cheese
  Salt and black pepper
- 1 package (about 16 ounces) fusilli pasta, cooked and drained
- 3 cups (12 ounces) shredded mozzarella cheese
- ½ cup grated Parmesan cheese

1. Preheat oven to 375°F. Line 2 baking sheets with foil. Place eggplant, peppers and onion, cut side down, on prepared baking sheets. Brush with olive oil; roast 30 minutes or until tender. Let cool; cut vegetables into bite-size pieces.

2. Combine ricotta cheese and vegetables in large bowl; season with salt and pepper. Add pasta; stir just until combined.

3. Spoon half of pasta mixture into 13×9-inch baking dish. Sprinkle with half of mozzarella and Parmesan cheeses. Repeat layers. Bake 25 minutes or until bubbly and browned.

Baked Fusilli with Roasted Vegetables

Four-Cheese Spicy Beefy Noodles

Makes 6 servings

1½ pounds ground beef
1 small onion, minced
1 clove garlic, minced
1 tablespoon chili powder
1 teaspoon paprika
⅛ teaspoon *each* dried basil, dried dill weed, dried thyme and
     dried marjoram
   Salt and black pepper
1 can (about 14 ounces) diced tomatoes with green chiles
1 can (8 ounces) tomato sauce
1 cup water
3 tablespoons Worcestershire sauce
1 package (about 10 ounces) egg noodles
½ cup (2 ounces) *each* shredded Cheddar, mozzarella, pepper jack
     and provolone cheeses

1. Brown beef, onion and garlic in large skillet over medium-high heat, stirring to break up meat; drain fat. Stir in chili powder, paprika, basil, dill, thyme and marjoram; cook and stir 2 minutes. Season with salt and pepper.

2. Add tomatoes, tomato sauce, water and Worcestershire sauce; mix well. Cover; simmer 20 minutes.

3. Cook noodles according to package directions. Drain well; cover and keep warm.

4. Combine meat mixture and noodles in 2-quart microwavable casserole. Combine cheeses and sprinkle evenly over top.

5. Microwave on HIGH 3 minutes. Let stand 5 minutes. Microwave 3 minutes more or until cheeses melt.

Four-Cheese Spicy Beefy Noodles

Shortcut Mac & Cheese

Easy Cheese & Tomato Macaroni

Makes 6 to 8 servings

2 packages (about 7 ounces each) macaroni and cheese dinner
1 tablespoon olive or vegetable oil
1 cup finely chopped onion
1 cup thinly sliced celery
1 can (28 ounces) CONTADINA® Recipe Ready Crushed Tomatoes
   Grated Parmesan cheese (optional)
   Sliced green onion or celery leaves (optional)

1. Cook macaroni (from macaroni and cheese dinner) according to package directions; drain.

2. Heat oil in large skillet. Add chopped onion and celery; sauté for 3 minutes or until vegetables are tender.

3. Combine tomatoes and cheese mixes from dinners in small bowl. Stir into vegetable mixture.

4. Simmer for 3 to 4 minutes or until mixture is thickened and heated through. Add macaroni to skillet; stir until well coated with sauce. Heat thoroughly, stirring occasionally. Sprinkle with Parmesan cheese and sliced green onion, if desired.

PREP TIME: 5 minutes
COOK TIME: 15 minutes

Cheesy Chicken & Broccoli Fettuccine

1 to 2 tablespoons olive oil
1 pound boneless skinless chicken breasts, cut into 1-inch pieces
2 boxes (10 ounces each) frozen broccoli with cheese sauce, thawed
1 package (9 ounces) refrigerated fettuccine, cooked and drained
Salt and black pepper

1. Heat oil in large skillet over medium-high heat. Add chicken; cook and stir 10 minutes or until no longer pink in center.

2. Stir in broccoli and cheese sauce; cook until heated through.

3. Add fettuccine; stir until well coated with cheese mixture. Season with salt and pepper.

Fastest Homemade Mac 'n' Cheese

1 can (10¾ ounces) CAMPBELL'S® Condensed Cheddar Cheese Soup
½ soup can milk
½ soup can water
1 cup uncooked elbow macaroni

1. Heat the soup, milk and water in a 2-quart saucepan over medium heat to a boil.

2. Add the macaroni and stir. Reduce the heat to low. Cook for 10 minutes or until the macaroni is tender but still firm, stirring often.

Cheesy Chicken & Broccoli Fettuccine

Mac & Cheese Toss

Makes 4 servings

8 ounces oven baked deli ham, diced
4 cups (1 quart) prepared deli macaroni and cheese
½ cup thawed frozen green peas
¼ cup milk or cream

MICROWAVE DIRECTIONS

1. Combine all ingredients in microwavable 2-quart casserole. Toss gently to blend.

2. Cover. Microwave on HIGH 3 minutes; stir. Microwave 1 minute more or until heated through.

TIP: To thaw peas quickly, place them in a small colander under cold running water 15 to 20 seconds or until thawed. Drain.

Mac & Cheese Toss

3-Cheese Chicken & Noodles

Makes 6 servings

3 cups chopped cooked chicken
1½ cups cottage cheese
1 can (10¾ ounces) condensed cream of chicken soup, undiluted
1 package (8 ounces) wide egg noodles, cooked and drained
1 cup (4 ounces) shredded Monterey Jack cheese
1 can (4 ounces) sliced mushrooms, drained
½ cup grated Parmesan cheese
½ cup diced onion
½ cup diced celery
½ cup diced green bell pepper
½ cup diced red bell pepper
½ cup chicken broth
2 tablespoons butter, melted
½ teaspoon dried thyme

SLOW COOKER DIRECTIONS

Combine all ingredients in slow cooker; mix well. Cover; cook on LOW 6 to 8 hours or on HIGH 3 to 4 hours.

TIP: This tasty dish is a great way to make a satisfying meal out of leftover chicken. You can even substitute cooked turkey for the chicken for a handy way to use up Thanksgiving leftovers.

3-Cheese Chicken & Noodles

South-of-the-Border Mac and Cheese

Makes 5 servings

1 package (about 7 ounces) macaroni and cheese dinner
1 pound ground sirloin beef
1 can (10 ounces) RO*TEL® Original Diced Tomatoes & Green Chilies,
    undrained
1 cup shredded Cheddar cheese, optional

1. Prepare macaroni and cheese in large saucepan according to package directions, omitting milk.

2. Brown beef in a large skillet over medium-high heat while macaroni cooks; drain. Add undrained tomatoes; mix well. Reduce heat to low; simmer 5 minutes, stirring occasionally.

3. Add beef mixture to prepared macaroni and cheese; sprinkle with Cheddar cheese, if desired.

COOK TIME: 15 minutes

South-of-the-Border Mac & Cheese

Skillet Lasagna

Makes 4 servings

1 pound ground beef
1 jar (1 pound 10 ounces) PREGO® Traditional Italian Sauce
½ cup ricotta cheese
½ cup shredded mozzarella cheese
¼ cup grated Parmesan cheese
4 cups medium egg noodles, cooked and drained

1. Cook the beef in a 12-inch skillet over medium-high heat until well browned, stirring frequently to break up meat. Pour off any fat.

2. Stir the sauce, cheeses and noodles into the skillet. Reduce the heat to medium. Cook and stir until hot and bubbling. Serve with additional Parmesan cheese.

For Meatier Skillet Lasagna: Use PREGO® Italian Sausage & Garlic Italian Sauce for the PREGO® Traditional Italian Sauce.

PREP TIME: 15 minutes
COOK TIME: 10 minutes

Skillet Lasagna

No-Fuss Macaroni & Cheese

Makes 6 to 8 servings

8 ounces uncooked elbow macaroni
4 ounces reduced-fat pasteurized processed cheese, cubed
1 cup (4 ounces) shredded Cheddar cheese
½ teaspoon salt
⅛ teaspoon black pepper
1½ cups milk

SLOW COOKER DIRECTIONS

Combine macaroni, cheeses, salt and pepper in slow cooker. Pour milk over top. Cover; cook on LOW 2 to 3 hours, stirring after 30 minutes.

Variation: Stir in sliced hot dogs or your favorite cooked vegetable.

PREP TIME: 10 minutes
COOK TIME: 2 to 3 hours

TIP: As with all macaroni and cheese dishes, as it sits, the cheese sauce thickens and begins to dry out. If it dries out, stir in a little extra milk and heat through. Do not cook longer than 4 hours.

No-Fuss Macaroni & Cheese

Cheeseburger Pasta

Makes 4 servings

    1 pound ground beef
    1 can CAMPBELL'S® Condensed Cheddar Cheese Soup
    1 can (10¾ ounces) CAMPBELL'S® Condensed Tomato Soup
1½ cups water
    2 cups uncooked medium shell-shaped pasta

1. Cook the beef in a 10-inch skillet over medium-high heat until the beef is well browned, stirring frequently to break up meat. Pour off any fat.

2. Stir the soups, water and pasta into the skillet. Heat to a boil. Reduce heat to medium. Cook for 10 minutes or until the pasta is tender but still firm, stirring often.

PREP TIME: 5 minutes
COOK TIME: 20 minutes

Cheeseburger Pasta

Spicy Sausage Mac & Cheese Bake

Makes 4 to 6 servings

3 hot Italian sausage links (about 1 pound)
¼ cup water
1 package (14 ounces) deluxe macaroni and cheese dinner
Salt and black pepper
1½ cups (6 ounces) shredded sharp Cheddar cheese

1. Preheat oven to 350°F. Spray 2-quart baking dish with nonstick cooking spray.

2. Place sausages in medium nonstick skillet; add water. Heat over medium heat; cover and simmer 10 to 12 minutes. Remove cover; brown sausages on all sides. Remove from heat. When cool enough to handle, cut sausages in half lengthwise and then into ½-inch pieces.

3. Prepare macaroni and cheese according to package directions. Stir in sausage pieces. Season with salt and pepper.

4. Spoon half of macaroni mixture into prepared baking dish. Sprinkle with ¾ cup cheese. Top with remaining half of macaroni mixture and remaining ¾ cup cheese. Bake 10 to 12 minutes or until heated through.

 TIP: You can substitute mild Italian sausage for the hot Italian sausage if you prefer a dish with less kick. You can also try turkey or chicken Italian sausage if they are available in your supermarket.

Spicy Sausage Mac & Cheese Bake

Lit'l Smokies 'n' Macaroni 'n' Cheese

Makes 8 servings

> 1 package (about 7 ounces) macaroni and cheese mix, prepared
>   according to package directions
> 1 pound HILLSHIRE FARM® Lit'l Smokies
> 1 can (10¾ ounces) condensed cream of celery or mushroom soup,
>   undiluted
> ⅓ cup milk
> 1 tablespoon minced parsley (optional)
> 1 cup (4 ounces) shredded Cheddar cheese

Preheat oven to 350°F.

Combine prepared macaroni and cheese, Lit'l Smokies, soup, milk and parsley, if desired, in medium bowl. Pour into small greased casserole. Sprinkle Cheddar cheese over top. Bake, uncovered, 20 minutes or until heated through.

Lit'l Smokies 'n' Macaroni 'n' Cheese

Fake 'Em Out Ravioli Lasagna

Makes 6 servings

> **Vegetable cooking spray**
> **1 jar (27 ounces) PREGO® Italian Sausage & Garlic Italian Sauce**
> **½ cup water**
> **1 package (30 ounces) frozen regular size cheese-filled ravioli (about 30 to 34)**
> **1½ cups shredded mozzarella cheese (6 ounces)**
> **Grated Parmesan cheese and chopped fresh parsley for garnish**

1. Heat the oven to 375°F. Spray a 13×9×2-inch baking dish with the cooking spray.

2. Stir the Italian sauce and water in a large bowl. Spread **1 cup** of the pasta sauce in the prepared dish. Top with ½ of the ravioli, **¾ cup** of the mozzarella cheese and **1 cup** of the pasta sauce. Top with the remaining ravioli and pasta sauce. Cover the dish with foil.

3. Bake for 35 minutes or until hot.

4. Uncover the dish and top with the remaining mozzarella cheese. Bake for 10 minutes more or until hot and bubbly. Let the lasagna stand for 10 minutes before serving. Garnish with the Parmesan cheese and parsley.

PREP TIME: 10 minutes
BAKE TIME: 45 minutes

Fake 'Em Out Ravioli Lasagna

Beyond Mac & Cheese

Creamy Chicken and Spinach Lasagna

Makes 4 servings

1¼ cups (6 ounces) shredded Swiss or mozzarella cheese, divided
1 cup ricotta cheese
1 teaspoon dried oregano
¼ teaspoon red pepper flakes
1 container (10 ounces) refrigerated Alfredo-style pasta sauce
⅓ cup water
4 no-boil lasagna noodles
1 package (10 ounces) frozen chopped spinach, thawed and squeezed dry
¼ cup grated Parmesan cheese
1½ cups cooked diced chicken

SLOW COOKER DIRECTIONS

1. Combine 1 cup Swiss cheese, ricotta cheese, oregano and pepper flakes in small bowl.

2. Blend pasta sauce with water in another small bowl.

3. Coat slow cooker with nonstick cooking spray. Break 2 lasagna noodles in half and place on bottom. Spread half of ricotta mixture over noodles. Layer with half of spinach, half of chicken and half of Parmesan cheese. Pour half of sauce mixture over top. Repeat layers.

4. Cover; cook on LOW 3 hours. Sprinkle remaining ¼ cup Swiss cheese on top. Cover and let stand 5 minutes or until cheese is melted.

PREP TIME: 20 minutes
COOK TIME: 3 hours

Broccoli and Provolone Stuffed Shells

Makes 6 to 8 servings

24 jumbo pasta shells
1 (10-ounce) package frozen chopped broccoli, thawed
1 cup BELGIOIOSO® Ricotta Cheese
½ cup shredded BELGIOIOSO® Provolone Cheese
1 tablespoon shredded onion
½ teaspoon dried basil
½ teaspoon dried oregano
   Salt and pepper to taste
1 (28-ounce) can crushed tomatoes

Preheat oven to 375°F. Prepare pasta according to directions until al dente. Drain and set aside. In large bowl, combine the remaining ingredients except tomatoes.

Pour about 1 cup tomatoes over bottom of 13×9-inch baking pan, breaking up tomatoes with fork. Spoon 1 tablespoon cheese mixture into each shell and place open-side-up in single layer in baking pan. Pour remaining tomatoes over and around shells. Cover pan with foil. Bake 25 to 30 minutes or until heated through.

Broccoli and Provolone Stuffed Shells

Pesto Lasagna

Makes 8 servings

1 package (16 ounces) uncooked lasagna noodles
3 tablespoons olive oil
1½ cups chopped onions
3 cloves garlic, finely chopped
3 packages (10 ounces each) frozen chopped spinach, thawed and
    squeezed dry
   Salt and black pepper
3 cups (24 ounces) ricotta cheese
1½ cups prepared pesto sauce
¾ cup grated Parmesan cheese
½ cup pine nuts, toasted*
4 cups (16 ounces) shredded mozzarella cheese
   Roasted red pepper strips (optional)

*To toast pine nuts, spread in single layer on baking sheet. Bake in preheated 350°F oven 5 to 7 minutes or until golden brown, stirring frequently.

1. Preheat oven to 350°F. Spray 13×9-inch casserole or lasagna pan with nonstick cooking spray. Partially cook lasagna noodles according to package directions.

2. Heat oil in large skillet over medium-high heat. Cook and stir onions and garlic until translucent. Add spinach; cook and stir about 5 minutes. Season with salt and pepper. Transfer to large bowl.

3. Add ricotta cheese, pesto, Parmesan cheese and pine nuts to spinach mixture; mix well.

4. Layer 5 lasagna noodles, slightly overlapping, in prepared casserole. Top with one third of ricotta mixture and one third of mozzarella. Repeat layers twice.

5. Bake 35 minutes or until bubbly. Garnish with red bell pepper strips.

Pesto Lasagna

Four-Cheese Manicotti

Makes 6 servings

    1 container (15 ounces) ricotta cheese
    2 cups (8 ounces) shredded mozzarella cheese
    ½ cup cottage cheese
    2 eggs, beaten
    2 tablespoons grated Parmesan cheese
    ½ teaspoon minced garlic
      Salt and black pepper
    1 package (about 8 ounces) uncooked manicotti shells
    1 pound ground beef
    1 jar (26 ounces) pasta sauce
    2 cups water

1. Preheat oven to 375°F.

2. Combine ricotta cheese, mozzarella cheese, cottage cheese, eggs, Parmesan cheese and garlic in large bowl; mix well. Season with salt and pepper. Fill manicotti shells with cheese mixture; place in 13×9-inch baking dish.

3. Brown beef in large skillet over medium-high heat, stirring to break up meat; drain fat. Stir in pasta sauce and water (mixture will be thin). Pour sauce over filled manicotti shells.

4. Cover with foil. Bake 1 hour or until sauce is thickened and shells are tender.

Four-Cheese Manicotti

Vegetarian Lasagna

Makes 4 to 6 servings

1 small eggplant, sliced into ½-inch-thick rounds
½ teaspoon salt
2 tablespoons olive oil, divided
1 tablespoon butter
8 ounces sliced mushrooms
1 small onion, diced
1 jar (26 ounces) pasta sauce
1 teaspoon dried basil
1 teaspoon dried oregano
2 cups ricotta cheese
1½ cups (6 ounces) shredded Monterey Jack cheese
1 cup grated Parmesan cheese, divided
1 package (8 ounces) whole wheat lasagna noodles, cooked and drained
1 medium zucchini, thinly sliced

SLOW COOKER DIRECTIONS

1. Sprinkle eggplant with salt; let stand 10 to 15 minutes. Rinse and pat dry. Brush with 1 tablespoon oil. Working in batches, brown both sides in large skillet over medium heat. Remove from skillet.

2. Heat remaining 1 tablespoon oil and butter in same skillet over medium heat; cook and stir mushrooms and onion until softened. Stir in pasta sauce, basil and oregano.

3. Combine ricotta cheese, Monterey Jack cheese and ½ cup Parmesan cheese in medium bowl.

4. Spread one third of sauce mixture in bottom of slow cooker. Layer with one third of lasagna noodles, half of eggplant and half of cheese mixture. Repeat layers once. Top with remaining third of lasagna noodles, zucchini, sauce mixture and ½ cup Parmesan.

5. Cover; cook on LOW 6 hours. Let stand 15 minutes before serving.

Mac and Cheese Bundles

Makes 8 bundles

2 cups cooked elbow macaroni
4 ounces American cheese, cubed
¼ cup half-and-half
½ cup diced ham
1 can (15 ounces) VEG•ALL® Original Mixed Vegetables, drained
1 tube (16 ounces) jumbo butter-flavored biscuit dough (8 biscuits)
1 large egg, lightly beaten

Preheat oven to 375°F.

Combine all ingredients except biscuit dough and egg in microwave-safe bowl. Microwave on high 2 minutes or until cheese is melted. Stir until pasta is well coated. Set aside to cool.

Roll out biscuits to ⅛-inch thickness. Spoon about ⅓ cup cooled macaroni mixture into center of each biscuit. Bring corners together and pinch to seal.

Brush bundles with egg. Bake 15 to 20 minutes or until golden brown.

TIP: Kids and adults will both love these all-in-one treats. Serve them at dinner with a salad or surprise your guests by serving them as an appetizer at your next party.

Slow Cooker Pizza Casserole

Makes 6 servings

1½ pounds ground beef
1 pound bulk pork sausage
4 jars (14 ounces each) pizza sauce
2 cups (8 ounces) shredded mozzarella cheese
2 cups grated Parmesan cheese
2 cans (4 ounces each) mushroom stems and pieces, drained
2 packages (3 ounces each) sliced pepperoni
½ cup finely chopped onion
½ cup finely chopped green bell pepper
1 clove garlic, minced
1 pound corkscrew pasta, cooked and drained

SLOW COOKER DIRECTIONS

1. Brown beef and sausage in large nonstick skillet over medium-high heat, stirring to break up meat; drain fat. Transfer meat to slow cooker. Add pizza sauce, cheeses, mushrooms, pepperoni, onion, bell pepper and garlic; mix well.

2. Cover; cook on LOW 3½ hours or on HIGH 2 hours. Stir in pasta. Cover; cook 15 to 20 minutes or until heated through.

Slow Cooker Pizza Casserole

Pesto Lasagna Rolls

Makes 8 servings

2 cups fresh basil leaves
2 cloves garlic
¾ cup (3 ounces) **SARGENTO® Artisan Blends™ Shredded Parmesan Cheese, divided**
¾ cup olive oil
2 cups (15 ounces) **SARGENTO® Whole Milk Ricotta Cheese***
1 cup (4 ounces) **SARGENTO® Shredded Reduced Fat Mozzarella Cheese**
1 egg, beaten
1 cup diced zucchini
16 lasagna noodles, cooked, drained and cooled

SARGENTO® Part-Skim Ricotta, Light Ricotta or Fat Free Ricotta can also be used.

Prepare pesto sauce in covered blender or food processor by processing basil with garlic until chopped. Add ½ cup Parmesan cheese; process until well mixed. With machine running, slowly add oil and continue processing until smooth. Set aside. In medium bowl, combine Ricotta and Mozzarella cheeses, remaining ¼ cup Parmesan cheese and egg; blend well. Fold in zucchini. Spread 2 heaping tablespoons cheese mixture on each lasagna noodle. Roll up each noodle individually and stand vertically in greased 11×7-inch baking dish. Pour pesto sauce over lasagna rolls; cover and bake at 350°F 40 minutes or until bubbly and heated through.

Pesto Lasagna Rolls

Spinach Ricotta Gnocchi

Makes 6 servings

> 1 package (16 ounces) frozen dumpling-shaped pasta (gnocchi)
> 2 cups frozen cut leaf spinach
> 1½ cups PREGO® Onion & Garlic *or* Traditional Italian Sauce
> ¼ cup grated Romano cheese
> ½ cup ricotta cheese
> 1 cup shredded mozzarella cheese (4 ounces)

1. Prepare the pasta according to the package directions in a 6-quart saucepot. Add the spinach during the last 3 minutes of cooking. Drain the pasta and spinach well in a colander. Return them to the saucepot.

2. Stir the sauce, Romano cheese and ricotta cheese into the saucepot. Heat, stirring occasionally, until hot and bubbling. Top with the mozzarella cheese.

PREP TIME: 5 minutes
COOK TIME: 25 minutes

TIP: Gnocchi are small dumplings typically made from potatoes that have been cooked and mashed. Tender and airy, they are an alternative to regular pasta and are widely available in the freezer case or in vaccuum-packed bags on the shelf in the pasta aisle of your supermarket.

Spinach Ricotta Gnocchi

Lasagna Supreme

Makes 8 to 10 servings

8 ounces uncooked lasagna noodles
½ pound mild Italian sausage, casings removed
½ pound ground beef
1 medium onion, chopped
2 cloves garlic, minced
1 can (about 14 ounces) whole tomatoes, undrained and chopped
1 can (6 ounces) tomato paste
2 teaspoons dried basil
1 teaspoon dried marjoram
1 can (4 ounces) sliced mushrooms, drained
2 eggs
2 cups cream-style cottage cheese
¾ cup grated Parmesan cheese, divided
2 tablespoons dried parsley flakes
½ teaspoon salt
½ teaspoon black pepper
2 cups (8 ounces) shredded Cheddar cheese
3 cups (12 ounces) shredded mozzarella cheese

1. Cook lasagna noodles according to package directions. Drain well; cover and keep warm.

2. Brown sausage, ground beef, onion and garlic in large skillet over medium-high heat, stirring to break up meat; drain fat.

3. Add tomatoes, tomato paste, basil and marjoram. Reduce heat to low. Cover; simmer 15 minutes, stirring often. Stir in mushrooms; set aside.

4. Preheat oven to 375°F. Beat eggs in large bowl. Add cottage cheese, ½ cup Parmesan cheese, parsley, salt and pepper; mix well.

5. Place half of noodles in bottom of greased 13×9-inch baking pan. Spread half of cottage cheese mixture over noodles, then half of meat mixture, half of Cheddar cheese and half of mozzarella cheese. Repeat layers. Top with remaining ¼ cup Parmesan cheese.

6. Bake 40 to 45 minutes or until bubbly. Let stand 15 minutes before serving.

Tip: Lasagna can be assembled, covered and refrigerated up to 2 days in advance. Bake, uncovered, in preheated 375°F oven 1 hour or until bubbly.

Lasagna Supreme

Crabmeat Manicotti

Makes 6 servings

> 12 pasta manicotti tubes
> 2 cups grated CABOT® 50% Reduced Fat Cheddar (about 8 ounces), divided
> 1½ cups CABOT® No Fat Cottage Cheese
> 6 ounces fresh crabmeat, flaked
> 2 tablespoons minced fresh parsley
> 1 tablespoon minced onion
> 1 teaspoon dried basil
>   Salt and ground black pepper to taste
> 2½ cups tomato sauce, divided

1. Preheat oven to 375°F.

2. Cook manicotti tubes according to package directions; drain thoroughly.

3. In medium bowl, combine 1 cup of cheddar, cottage cheese, crabmeat, parsley, onion and basil. Season with salt and pepper. Fill manicotti tubes with mixture.

4. Pour 2 cups of tomato sauce over bottom of shallow baking dish. Arrange manicotti on top. Spoon remaining ½ cup sauce over manicotti. Cover dish tightly with foil.

5. Bake for 25 minutes. Uncover dish, sprinkle remaining 1 cup cheddar over top, and return to oven for 5 minutes to melt cheese.

Variation: For Florentine version, substitute 1 (10-ounce) package frozen chopped spinach, thawed and squeezed dry, for crabmeat.

Taco Pasta Casserole

Makes 6 servings

8 ounces uncooked rotini pasta
1 pound ground beef
2 cloves garlic, minced
1 (15-ounce) can tomato sauce
⅔ cup whole kernel corn
⅓ cup diced red bell pepper
1 (1¼-ounce) package taco seasoning
2 tablespoons water
1 teaspoon dried oregano
1 cup shredded colby-jack cheese, divided
½ cup reduced-fat sour cream

Cook pasta according to package directions; drain.

In large nonstick skillet, brown ground beef and garlic; drain thoroughly. Stir in tomato sauce, corn, bell pepper, taco seasoning, water and oregano. Bring to a boil and simmer 5 minutes.

Combine pasta, ½ cup cheese and sour cream. Spoon into 2-quart baking dish coated with nonstick cooking spray. Top with meat mixture and remaining ½ cup cheese. Bake uncovered at 350°F for 30 minutes.

Favorite recipe from *North Dakota Wheat Commission*

Spicy Lasagna Rollers

Makes 6 servings

1½ pounds Italian sausage, casings removed
1 jar (28 ounces) pasta sauce, divided
1 can (8 ounces) tomato sauce
½ cup chopped roasted red pepper
¾ teaspoon Italian seasoning
½ teaspoon red pepper flakes
1 container (15 ounces) ricotta cheese
1 package (10 ounces) frozen chopped spinach, thawed and
    squeezed dry
2 cups (8 ounces) shredded Italian cheese blend, divided
1 cup (4 ounces) shredded Cheddar cheese, divided
1 egg, lightly beaten
12 lasagna noodles, cooked and drained

1. Preheat oven to 350°F. Spray 13×9-inch baking pan with nonstick cooking spray.

2. Brown sausage in large skillet over medium heat, stirring to break up meat; drain fat. Stir in ½ cup pasta sauce, tomato sauce, roasted red pepper, seasoning and pepper flakes.

3. Combine ricotta cheese, spinach, 1½ cups Italian cheese blend, ½ cup Cheddar cheese and egg in medium bowl. Spread ¼ cup ricotta mixture over each noodle. Top with ⅓ cup sausage mixture. Tightly roll up each noodle from short end. Place rolls, seam sides down, in prepared baking pan. Pour remaining pasta sauce over rolls. Sprinkle with remaining ½ cup Italian cheese blend and ½ cup Cheddar cheese. Cover pan with foil.

4. Bake 30 minutes. Carefully remove foil; bake 15 minutes or until bubbly.

Spicy Lasagna Rollers

Seafood Lasagna

Makes 8 to 10 servings

1 package (16 ounces) uncooked lasagna noodles
2 tablespoons butter
1 large onion, finely chopped
1 package (8 ounces) cream cheese, cut into ½-inch pieces, softened
1½ cups cream-style cottage cheese
1 egg, lightly beaten
2 teaspoons dried basil
½ teaspoon salt
⅛ teaspoon black pepper
1 egg, lightly beaten
2 cans (10¾ ounces each) cream of mushroom soup, undiluted
⅓ cup milk
1 clove garlic, minced
½ pound bay scallops, rinsed and patted dry
½ pound flounder fillets, rinsed, patted dry and cut into ½-inch cubes
½ pound medium raw shrimp, peeled
½ cup dry white wine
1 cup (4 ounces) shredded mozzarella cheese
2 tablespoons grated Parmesan cheese

1. Cook lasagna noodles according to package directions. Drain well; cover and keep warm.

2. Melt butter in large skillet over medium heat. Add onion; cook and stir until tender. Stir in cream cheese, cottage cheese, egg, basil, salt and pepper; mix well.

3. Combine soups, milk and garlic in large bowl until well blended. Stir in scallops, flounder, shrimp and wine.

4. Preheat oven to 350°F. Grease 13×9-inch baking pan.

5. Place layer of lasagna noodles in prepared pan, overlapping edges. Spread half of cheese mixture over noodles. Place layer of noodles over cheese mixture and top with half of seafood mixture. Repeat layers. Sprinkle with mozzarella and Parmesan cheeses.

6. Bake 45 minutes or until bubbly. Let stand 15 minutes before serving.

The publisher would like to thank the companies and organizations listed below for the use of their recipes and photographs in this publication.

BelGioioso® Cheese Inc.

Bob Evans®

Cabot® Creamery Cooperative

Campbell Soup Company

ConAgra Foods®

Cream of Wheat® Cereal

Del Monte Corporation

Hillshire Farm®

Hormel Foods, LLC

©2009 Kraft Foods, KRAFT, KRAFT Hexagon Logo, PHILADELPHIA AND PHILADELPHIA Logo are registered trademarks of Kraft Foods Holdings, Inc. All rights reserved.

Nestlé USA

North Dakota Wheat Commission

Reckitt Benckiser Inc.

Sargento® Foods Inc.

Veg•All®

Wisconsin Milk Marketing Board

A

Asparagus
Chicken Asparagus Gratin, 49
Creamy Fettuccine with Asparagus & Lima Beans, 20
Fettuccine with Gorgonzola Sauce, 88

B
Baked Fusilli with Roasted Vegetables, 90
Baked Macaroni & Cheese, 64
Baked Pasta with Ricotta, 58
Baked Rigatoni, 52
Beans
Creamy Fettuccine with Asparagus & Lima Beans, 20
Pasta & White Bean Casserole, 78
Tuscan Baked Rigatoni, 84
Beef, Ground
Beef and Veg•All® Cheddar Bake, 34
Beefy Cheddar Rotini, 86
Cheeseburger Pasta, 108
Four-Cheese Manicotti, 122
Four-Cheese Spicy Beefy Noodles, 92
Lasagna Supreme, 132
Layered Pasta Casserole, 32
No-Chop Pastitsio, 70
Pizza Casserole, 76
Skillet Lasagna, 104
Slow Cooker Pizza Casserole, 126
South-of-the-Border Mac and Cheese, 102
Southwestern Skillet Macaroni, 12
Taco Pasta Casserole, 135
Beefy Cheddar Rotini, 86
Broccoli
Beefy Cheddar Rotini, 86
Broccoli and Pasta Bianco, 68
Broccoli and Provolone Stuffed Shells, 118
Broccoli Mac & Cheese, 48
Cheesy Chicken & Broccoli Fettuccine, 96
Spicy Jac Mac & Cheese with Broccoli, 72

C
Cauliflower Mac & Gouda, 36
Cheese (see also individual listings)
Cauliflower Mac & Gouda, 36
Cheesy Chicken-Orzo Skillet, 26
Creamy 3-Cheese Pasta, 46

Cheese (continued)
Four-Cheese Mac & Cheese, 34
Mac & Mornay, 12
Pasta & White Bean Casserole, 78
Spicy Lasagna Rollers, 136
Taco Pasta Casserole, 135
3-Cheese Baked Ham & Tortellini, 50
Three-Pepper Fettuccine, 14
Cheese, American
Chile-Cheese Rotini, 82
Creamy Confetti Macaroni, 60
Four-Cheese Mac & Cheese, 34
Mac and Cheese Bundles, 125
Cheese, Cheddar
Baked Macaroni & Cheese, 64
Beef and Veg•All® Cheddar Bake, 34
Beefy Cheddar Rotini, 86
Broccoli Mac & Cheese, 48
Cheeseburger Pasta, 108
Cheesy Tuna Noodle Casserole, 40
Chicken Asparagus Gratin, 49
Chile-Cheese Rotini, 82
Crabmeat Manicotti, 134
Enlightened Macaroni and Cheese, 65
Fastest Homemade Mac 'n' Cheese, 96
Four-Cheese Mac & Cheese, 34
Four-Cheese Spicy Beefy Noodles, 92
Italian Three-Cheese Macaroni, 38
Lasagna Supreme, 132
Linguine with Chipotle Cheddar and Red Peppers, 89
Lit'l Smokies 'n' Macaroni 'n' Cheese, 112
Macaroni & Cheese with Bacon, 62
No-Fuss Macaroni & Cheese, 106
Not Your Gramma's Kugel, 74
Pennsylvania Dutch Ham & Noodle Casserole, 24
Rigatoni with Four Cheeses, 80
South-of-the-Border Mac and Cheese, 102
Southwestern Skillet Macaroni, 12
Spicy Jac Mac & Cheese with Broccoli, 72
Spicy Lasagna Rollers, 136
Spicy Sausage Mac & Cheese Bake, 110
Stovetop Macaroni and Cheese, 4

Cheese, Cheddar *(continued)*
Triple Cheese & Turkey Tetrazzini, 81
Tuna & Pasta Cheddar Melt, 30
Veggie Mac & Cheese, 44
Cheese, Cottage
Crabmeat Manicotti, 134
Creamy Confetti Macaroni, 60
Four-Cheese Manicotti, 122
Lasagna Supreme, 132
Not Your Gramma's Kugel, 74
Seafood Lasagna, 138
3-Cheese Chicken & Noodles, 100
Cheese, Cream
Chicken Tetrazzini, 39
Seafood Lasagna, 138
Cheese, Fontina
Pesto Chicken Mac & Cheese, 22
Tuscan Baked Rigatoni, 84
Cheese, Gorgonzola
Fettuccine with Gorgonzola Sauce, 88
Shells and Gorgonzola, 8
Cheese, Monterey Jack
Enlightened Macaroni and Cheese, 65
3-Cheese Chicken & Noodles, 100
Triple Cheese & Turkey Tetrazzini, 81
Vegetarian Lasagna, 124
Cheese, Mozzarella
Baked Fusilli with Roasted Vegetables, 90
Baked Pasta with Ricotta, 58
Baked Rigatoni, 52
Broccoli and Pasta Bianco, 68
Cheesy Artichoke-Chicken Rotini, 54
Fake 'Em Out Ravioli Lasagna, 114
Four-Cheese Mac & Cheese, 34
Four-Cheese Manicotti, 122
Four-Cheese Spicy Beefy Noodles, 92
Italian Three-Cheese Macaroni, 38
Lasagna Supreme, 132
Layered Pasta Casserole, 32
Penne with Roasted Tomato Sauce and Mozzarella, 18
Pesto Chicken Mac & Cheese, 22
Pesto Lasagna, 120
Pesto Lasagna Rolls, 128
Pizza Casserole, 76
Rigatoni with Four Cheeses, 80
Seafood Lasagna, 138

Cheese, Mozzarella *(continued)*
Skillet Lasagna, 104
Skillet Vegetable Lasgana, 16
Slow Cooker Pizza Casserole, 126
Spinach-Cheese Pasta Bake, 57
Spinach Ricotta Gnocchi, 130
Three-Cheese Baked Ziti with Spinach, 42
Cheese, Parmesan
Baked Fusilli with Roasted Vegetables, 90
Baked Pasta with Ricotta, 58
Chicken Tetrazzini, 39
Classic Fettuccine Alfredo, 28
Creamy Fettuccine with Asparagus & Lima Beans, 20
Creamy Fettuccine with Prosciutto and Peas, 73
Creamy 3-Cheese Pasta, 46
Fettuccine alla Carbonara, 6
Italian Three-Cheese Macaroni, 38
Lasagna Supreme, 132
Layered Pasta Casserole, 32
No-Chop Pastitsio, 70
Pesto Chicken Mac & Cheese, 22
Pesto Lasagna, 120
Pesto Lasagna Rolls, 128
Rigatoni with Four Cheeses, 80
Slow Cooker Pizza Casserole, 126
Spicy Jac Mac & Cheese with Broccoli, 72
Three-Cheese Baked Ziti with Spinach, 42
3-Cheese Chicken & Noodles, 100
Tuscan Baked Rigatoni, 84
Vegetarian Lasagna, 124
Veggie Mac & Cheese, 44
Cheese, Pasteurized Process
Country Sausage Macaroni and Cheese, 56
No-Fuss Macaroni & Cheese, 106
Cheese, Pepper Jack
Four-Cheese Spicy Beefy Noodles, 92
Southwestern Corn and Pasta Casserole, 66
Spicy Jac Mac & Cheese with Broccoli, 72
Cheese, Provolone
Broccoli and Provolone Stuffed Shells, 118
Four-Cheese Spicy Beefy Noodles, 92

Cheese, Ricotta
Baked Fusilli with Roasted
Vegetables, 90
Baked Pasta with Ricotta, 58
Broccoli and Provolone Stuffed
Shells, 118
Creamy Chicken and Spinach
Lasagna, 116
Four-Cheese Manicotti, 122
Layered Pasta Casserole, 32
Pesto Lasagna, 120
Pesto Lasagna Rolls, 128
Skillet Lasagna, 104
Skillet Vegetable Lasgana, 16
Spicy Lasagna Rollers, 136
Spinach-Cheese Pasta Bake, 57
Spinach Ricotta Gnocchi, 130
Three-Cheese Baked Ziti with
Spinach, 42
Vegetarian Lasagna, 124
Cheese, Swiss
Creamy Chicken and Spinach
Lasagna, 116
Creamy Confetti Macaroni, 60
Ham and Swiss Penne Skillet, 10
Cheeseburger Pasta, 108
Cheesy Artichoke-Chicken Rotini, 54
Cheesy Chicken & Broccoli Fettuccine,
96
Cheesy Chicken-Orzo Skillet, 26
Cheesy Tuna Noodle Casserole, 40
Chicken
Cheesy Artichoke-Chicken Rotini,
54
Cheesy Chicken & Broccoli
Fettuccine, 96
Cheesy Chicken-Orzo Skillet, 26
Chicken Asparagus Gratin, 49
Chicken Tetrazzini, 39
Creamy Chicken and Spinach
Lasagna, 116
Pesto Chicken Mac & Cheese, 22
3-Cheese Chicken & Noodles, 100
Chile-Cheese Rotini, 82
Classic Fettuccine Alfredo, 28
Corn
Ham and Swiss Penne Skillet, 10
Southwestern Corn and Pasta
Casserole, 66
Taco Pasta Casserole, 135
Country Sausage Macaroni and
Cheese, 56
Crabmeat Manicotti, 134
Creamy Chicken and Spinach
Lasagna, 116

Creamy Confetti Macaroni, 60
Creamy Fettuccine with Asparagus &
Lima Beans, 20
Creamy Fettuccine with Prosciutto and
Peas, 73
Creamy 3-Cheese Pasta, 46

E
Easy Cheese & Tomato Macaroni, 94
Eggplant
Baked Fusilli with Roasted
Vegetables, 90
Vegetarian Lasagna, 124
Enlightened Macaroni and Cheese, 65

F
Fake 'Em Out Ravioli Lasagna, 114
Fastest Homemade Mac 'n' Cheese, 96
Fettuccine alla Carbonara, 6
Fettuccine with Gorgonzola Sauce, 88
Fish and Shellfish
Cheesy Tuna Noodle Casserole, 40
Crabmeat Manicotti, 134
Seafood Lasagna, 138
Tuna & Pasta Cheddar Melt, 30
Four-Cheese Mac & Cheese, 34
Four-Cheese Manicotti, 122
Four-Cheese Spicy Beefy Noodles, 92

H
Ham
Creamy Fettuccine with Prosciutto
and Peas, 73
Ham and Swiss Penne Skillet, 10
Mac and Cheese Bundles, 125
Mac & Cheese Toss, 98
Pennsylvania Dutch Ham & Noodle
Casserole, 24
3-Cheese Baked Ham & Tortellini, 50

I
Italian Three-Cheese Macaroni, 38

L
Lasagna Supreme, 132
Layered Pasta Casserole, 32
Linguine with Chipotle Cheddar and
Red Peppers, 89
Lit'l Smokies 'n' Macaroni 'n' Cheese,
112

M
Mac and Cheese Bundles, 125
Mac & Cheese Toss, 98
Mac & Mornay, 12

Macaroni and Cheese Dinner
Easy Cheese & Tomato Macaroni, 94
Lit'l Smokies 'n' Macaroni 'n' Cheese, 112
South-of-the-Border Mac and Cheese, 102
Spicy Sausage Mac & Cheese Bake, 110
Macaroni & Cheese with Bacon, 62

N
No-Chop Pastitsio, 70
No-Fuss Macaroni & Cheese, 106
Not Your Gramma's Kugel, 74

P
Pasta & White Bean Casserole, 78
Peas
Cheesy Tuna Noodle Casserole, 40
Creamy Fettuccine with Prosciutto and Peas, 73
Ham and Swiss Penne Skillet, 10
Mac & Cheese Toss, 98
Penne with Roasted Tomato Sauce and Mozzarella, 18
Pennsylvania Dutch Ham & Noodle Casserole, 24
Pesto Chicken Mac & Cheese, 22
Pesto Lasagna, 120
Pesto Lasagna Rolls, 128
Pizza Casserole, 76

R
Rigatoni with Four Cheeses, 80

S
Sausage
Baked Rigatoni, 52
Country Sausage Macaroni and Cheese, 56
Lasagna Supreme, 132
Layered Pasta Casserole, 32
Lit'l Smokies 'n' Macaroni 'n' Cheese, 112
Penne with Roasted Tomato Sauce and Mozzarella, 18
Pizza Casserole, 76
Slow Cooker Pizza Casserole, 126
Spicy Lasagna Rollers, 136
Spicy Sausage Mac & Cheese Bake, 110
Tuscan Baked Rigatoni, 84
Seafood Lasagna, 138
Shells and Gorgonzola, 8

Skillet Lasagna, 104
Skillet Vegetable Lasgana, 16
Slow Cooker Recipes
Beefy Cheddar Rotini, 86
Chile-Cheese Rotini, 82
Creamy Chicken and Spinach Lasagna, 116
No-Fuss Macaroni & Cheese, 106
Not Your Gramma's Kugel, 74
Slow Cooker Pizza Casserole, 126
3-Cheese Chicken & Noodles, 100
Vegetarian Lasagna, 124
South-of-the-Border Mac and Cheese, 102
Southwestern Corn and Pasta Casserole, 66
Southwestern Skillet Macaroni, 12
Spicy Jac Mac & Cheese with Broccoli, 72
Spicy Lasagna Rollers, 136
Spicy Sausage Mac & Cheese Bake, 110
Spinach
Cheesy Chicken-Orzo Skillet, 26
Creamy Chicken and Spinach Lasagna, 116
Layered Pasta Casserole, 32
Pesto Chicken Mac & Cheese, 22
Pesto Lasagna, 120
Skillet Vegetable Lasgana, 16
Spicy Lasagna Rollers, 136
Spinach-Cheese Pasta Bake, 57
Spinach Ricotta Gnocchi, 130
Three-Cheese Baked Ziti with Spinach, 42
Tuscan Baked Rigatoni, 84
Stovetop Macaroni and Cheese, 4

T
Taco Pasta Casserole, 135
3-Cheese Baked Ham & Tortellini, 50
Three-Cheese Baked Ziti with Spinach, 42
3-Cheese Chicken & Noodles, 100
Three-Pepper Fettuccine, 14
Triple Cheese & Turkey Tetrazzini, 81
Tuna & Pasta Cheddar Melt, 30
Tuscan Baked Rigatoni, 84

V
Vegetarian Lasagna, 124
Veggie Mac & Cheese, 44

METRIC CONVERSION CHART

VOLUME MEASUREMENTS (dry)

1/8 teaspoon = 0.5 mL
1/4 teaspoon = 1 mL
1/2 teaspoon = 2 mL
3/4 teaspoon = 4 mL
1 teaspoon = 5 mL
1 tablespoon = 15 mL
2 tablespoons = 30 mL
1/4 cup = 60 mL
1/3 cup = 75 mL
1/2 cup = 125 mL
2/3 cup = 150 mL
3/4 cup = 175 mL
1 cup = 250 mL
2 cups = 1 pint = 500 mL
3 cups = 750 mL
4 cups = 1 quart = 1 L

VOLUME MEASUREMENTS (fluid)

1 fluid ounce (2 tablespoons) = 30 mL
4 fluid ounces (1/2 cup) = 125 mL
8 fluid ounces (1 cup) = 250 mL
12 fluid ounces (1 1/2 cups) = 375 mL
16 fluid ounces (2 cups) = 500 mL

WEIGHTS (mass)

1/2 ounce = 15 g
1 ounce = 30 g
3 ounces = 90 g
4 ounces = 120 g
8 ounces = 225 g
10 ounces = 285 g
12 ounces = 360 g
16 ounces = 1 pound = 450 g

DIMENSIONS

1/16 inch = 2 mm
1/8 inch = 3 mm
1/4 inch = 6 mm
1/2 inch = 1.5 cm
3/4 inch = 2 cm
1 inch = 2.5 cm

OVEN TEMPERATURES

250°F = 120°C
275°F = 140°C
300°F = 150°C
325°F = 160°C
350°F = 180°C
375°F = 190°C
400°F = 200°C
425°F = 220°C
450°F = 230°C

BAKING PAN SIZES

Utensil	Size in Inches/Quarts	Metric Volume	Size in Centimeters
Baking or Cake Pan (square or rectangular)	8×8×2	2 L	20×20×5
	9×9×2	2.5 L	23×23×5
	12×8×2	3 L	30×20×5
	13×9×2	3.5 L	33×23×5
Loaf Pan	8×4×3	1.5 L	20×10×7
	9×5×3	2 L	23×13×7
Round Layer Cake Pan	8×1½	1.2 L	20×4
	9×1½	1.5 L	23×4
Pie Plate	8×1¼	750 mL	20×3
	9×1¼	1 L	23×3
Baking Dish or Casserole	1 quart	1 L	—
	1½ quart	1.5 L	—
	2 quart	2 L	—